1/09 Ingram $9.95

138.2
GAB

UNEXPECTED INTIMACY

Everyday Connections
that Nourish the Soul

SARAH GABRIEL

my sane life
publications

Denver

WITHDRAWN
www.loneconelibrary.org

Norwood Public Library
1110 Lucerne Street
Norwood, CO 81423

NORWOOD PUBLIC LIBRARY

WD

3 9101 00022 1946

Copyright © 2009 by Sarah Gabriel

All rights reserved. No part of this book may be reproduced or transmitted in any form or by any means, electronic or mechanical, including photocopying, recording or by any information storage and retrieval system, without written permission from the author, except for the inclusion of brief quotation in review.

My Sane Life Publications
Great Room Press
P.O. Box 370441
Denver, CO 80237-0441
www.unexpectedintimacy.com
info@greatroompress.com

Cover by rk-design
Interior by Peter Altenberg

Library of Congress Control Number
2008931937

ISBN 978-0-9801656-1-6
0-9801656-1-X

Printed on recycled paper.
Printed in the United States of America

To David,
with profound love
and gratitude

WITHDRAWN
www.loneconelibrary.org

Contents

Acknowledgements

NATURALLY, A BOOK ABOUT INTIMATE connections has come into being because of the relationships I have had with so many wonderful people. First and foremost, I want to thank all my friends and family who have so open-heartedly agreed to let me tell our stories, and the many more whose stories nourish my soul. The form of the book evolved from my walking buddies and from my friends with whom I share deep Conversational Intimacy. I send waves of gratitude to members of my Family of Circumstance and my Family of Choice. You are each a blessing in my life.

The writing process is a universe of its own, and I want to thank Kerry Brazell, Sue Parker Gerson, Kathy Kehril and Debbie Zucker for joining me in that world. Jack, I thank you deeply for your goodwill and encouragement of the artist in me. There are authors and artists whose work I find inspirational—who break taboos, write real stories about themselves and what they see happening in the world with honesty and wit. As a result, they give us all permission to experience our own lives more fully and deeply. Just to name a few—Hans Selye, Natalie Goldberg, Barbara Kingsolver, Madeline Levine, Daniel Goleman, Reb Zalman Schachter-Shalomi, Mary Pipher, Anne Lamott, Elizabeth Gilbert, Mary Catherine Bateson and Thomas Friedman.

Our earliest learning and longest running intimate relationships are often with our family of origin. I want to thank mine—my sisters, Lisa and Marcy, for strong connections and the first-round edit that propelled me to the next level; Mom, for your eternal open-mindedness to all my ideas; and Dad, for your generosity that knows no end. David, you came into this world and cracked open my hard shell, exposing the inner softness to the light. Thanks for letting me print so many stories about you.

Preface to the 2nd Edition

ONE OF THE FIRST THINGS TO SUFFER FROM our fast-forward, busy-all-the-time culture is our relationships. Whether you are single or partnered, caught up in the frenzy or swimming against the tide, getting and staying connected has become more of a challenge. Readers of the 1st edition of *Unexpected Intimacy* asked for help—some simple and straightforward advice for developing and maintaining all kinds of healthy relationships. To that end, in this new edition, you'll find *Unexpected Intimacy Revealed: Strategies for Building Intimate Connections* in the back of the book. It is a 4-step E.A.S.Y. approach to building stronger relationships. Just as the stories in *Unexpected Intimacy* leave you with a clear sense of the ways in which you can be nourished by all your relationships, the strategies in *Unexpected Intimacy Revealed* guide you in bringing more vitality into your own personal constellation of connections.

We need both a fresh perspective on relationships and a straightforward way to strengthen our connections. Now, *Unexpected Intimacy* offers both.

Don't Skip the Prologue

The single most common finding from a half-century's research on the correlates of life satisfaction, not only in the United States but around the world, is that happiness is best predicted by the breadth and depth of one's social connections.

~ Robert Putnam, professor and author of
Bowling Alone: The Collapse and Revival of American Community

FIRST PREMISE: THERE'S TOO MUCH PRESSURE on "The One." In our culture, so much importance has been attached to finding the perfect partner—that man or woman who miraculously heals all our wounds and satisfies all our needs—that many of us end up either disappointed with our choice or feeling shame for being "alone." With fairy tales of *Cinderella* and *Sleeping Beauty* embedded in our cultural psyches, expectations of "Happily Ever After" are annoyingly beyond our reach. Nearly fifty percent of us are disappointed or annoyed enough to leave our current "ever after" to search for one with a better ending. Others of us choose to remain and live with disappointment for the sake of children, religious beliefs, economic realities, or other motivating factors. Still others of us simply remain single while yearning for our knight in shining armor (women) or our *geisha* (men), becoming depressed and ashamed because s/he hasn't shown up yet. Even those of us who have found our soul mate often exert too much pressure on that person to fulfill all of our needs for intimacy—to understand, appreciate, and connect with all that we hold dear.

This is just too much pressure on The One, and frankly, it's too little pressure on the rest of the people in our lives.

When I hear someone asking a single person if they are "in a relationship," It makes me want to scream, *"Of course they are in a relationship. Right now they are talking with you, so right now they are in a relationship with you!"*

Unexpected Intimacy is a call for a change in the way we view and value all our relationships. It is not a book about how to find your soul mate or about healing the wounds of relationships. It is rather a book of stories about opening up to more possibilities of nourishing your soul in unexpected ways. Instead of asking people about their marital status, let's inquire about their intimacy constellations —the evolving set of people in their lives— and how each relationship is valued.

SECOND PREMISE: THERE ARE A GROWING number of documented health and lifestyle benefits, presenting us with convincing reasons to focus on more than The One. Robert Putnam, in his book *Bowling Alone: The Collapse and Revival of American Community*, reports, "Statistically speaking, the evidence for the health consequences of social connectedness is as strong today as was the evidence for the health consequences of smoking at the time of the first surgeon general's report on smoking." He goes on to say that, "over the last twenty years, more than a dozen large studies of this sort in the US, Scandinavia and Japan have shown that people who are socially disconnected are between two and five times more likely to die from all causes, compared with matched individuals who have close ties with family, friends and community." Bowling alone, he says, may represent one of the nation's most serious public health challenges.

Mary Pipher, in her book *The Shelter of Each Other*, reports that, "Years ago a sociologist postulated that there was a critical number of social contacts that a person needed every week to stay sane. He speculated that unless seven familiar people 'interacted' with the person, he or she would be at risk for mental illness." Positive psychology researchers Martin Seligman and Ed Diener compared "very happy people" with less happy people and found that the only external factor that distinguished them was "rich and satisfying social relationships."

The benefits of nourishing and valuing all of our relationships—beyond The One—are clear. We are presented with relationship possibilities every day, but we often miss the opportunities because technology has lowered the need for face-to-face contact to get things done, American culture values independence and privacy over interdependence, and we are all involved in our own little busy worlds. Fortunately there is a simple, easy fix: Cultivate connections. With this, we build relationships. Without it, what we have is disconnection—a spiritual crisis of sorts—and a sense that we don't belong.

Okay, so "simple, easy fix" might be a bit optimistic. It is simple but it isn't always so easy because, as a society, we have developed a habit of disconnection. Here's what it sometimes looks like for me: I walk into the grocery store with my three canvas bags. I do my shopping. As I come through the line to the cashier, I hand her my three bags. She is holding them, and with a glazed look in her eyes, she asks no one in particular, "Paper or Plastic?" I look back at her, trying without success to catch her eye. "Not paper *or* plastic," I respond. "I have my own bags. I just handed them to you." Frustrated, I punctuate the exchange with, "You are holding them!" hoping to bring her attention to this here-and-now relationship. I point to my bags and eventually she makes the connection. The damage, however, is done. I leave the store in a state of existential angst, disoriented with thoughts like "What is this world coming to? Life is full of mindless routine, no one cares, no one feels connected. We are losing our ability to engage with life. We are all free-falling." Then, for the rest of the day, I don't get much done. Lots of wasted time ensues. It can take me hours to refocus. I'm not kidding. Disconnection turns my world topsy-turvy.

According to Dr. Amy Arnsten, a Professor of Neurobiology at Yale University, in her article, "The Biology of Being Frazzled," we've learned that this kind of experience handicaps our abilities for learning, for holding information in working memory, for reacting flexibly and creatively, for focusing attention at will, and for planning and organizing effectively. We can sum it up in two words: Cognitive Dysfunction.

So, doing a little self-coaching, I ask, "Where can I find an antidote to the frazzle of this Disconnection?" The answer: Make a connection. And then value the connection. If I were to engage with a couple of the employees in the store and also with the cashier—make some eye contact—I could avoid this frazzle. I'm pretty independent so I don't often need help in the store, but I could ask for help anyway. I could talk to the produce guy about what he recommends for stir-fry. I could ask the fish gal what came in fresh today or what seasoning to use to bring out the flavor. I could comment on the shirt the cashier is wearing or even chit-chat about the weather ....

Expected Outcome: Not only will I feel better about connecting, it is likely that the employees at the store will also feel more engaged with their work for having engaged with me about it. I'll be able to return to work refreshed and ready to re-engage. Ripples abound.

That's one thing I could do. I figured another thing I could do is write a book. So I did.

I wrote *Unexpected Intimacy* to help people both broaden their vision of intimacy and add value in everyday encounters so that our seven necessary interactions should be easily exceeded. The rapid changes in our culture make this a challenge. Asking questions, raising our awareness and sharing stories is a start. What follows are some of mine.

The Power of Naming

The process of knowing and being known is, potentially, never-ending, as there is always more that can be revealed, always more that can be discovered.

~ Tal Ben-Shahar, author of *Happier*

Grocery Store Intimacy

Each friend represents a world in us,
a world possibly not born until they arrive,
and it is only by this meeting that a new world is born.

~ Anaïs Nin, author

A FEW YEARS AGO, I UNEXPECTEDLY FOUND myself in the cleaning products aisle in the supermarket. I hadn't been in that aisle for years, not since I'd switched to more natural/organic products. However, I had a housemate who had just moved out and in her wake, she had left behind a half-inch of grime in the bathtub. Monica, my once-a-month cleaning lady, told me pretty clearly that my namby-pamby organic citrus stuff was not going to do the job. I was going to need something with power. In no uncertain terms, she insisted that I needed to buy real chemicals.

So there I was, oh-my-God trying to figure out which of the 600 bathroom cleaning products was best for my job. With bleach, without bleach, some kill odors, some kill bacteria, some go kaboom, and some claim to do it all. The situation triggered a severe case of existential angst. The choices so overwhelmed me that I became paralyzed.

At that moment, an old woman walked by. I'm going to guess that she was in her eighties—robust, but clearly an elder. She stopped when she saw me, and then she *really* saw me. She remarked, "Wouldn't it be nice if there were only two or three to choose from?"

Well, I wanted to kiss her. She had read my mind. Like a psychic she had heard my thoughts. She understood. At that moment, she knew me better than anyone else on the planet knew me. What we were experiencing was the "Desire for Simpler Times Intimacy" that she and I deeply shared in that moment. I was so nurtured by that encounter that my intimacy needs for the day were met.

Many people have a narrow view of what intimacy means. They think of it as something that is whispered and sexy—that to say a relationship is "intimate" means you've had your clothes off. If I say "intimate moment," what do you think of? Romantic dinner by candlelight? Gazing into the eyes of someone who later that evening you hope to see naked? Okay, Cinderella, I would agree that vision does describe an intimate moment, but that is only one type among hundreds of types of intimacy. Just as the Eskimos have lots of words for snow, we need more words for intimacy. Each relationship I have, indeed each encounter I experience, has the potential to satisfy some of my own unique human need for intimacy.

I define an intimate moment as any time one person sees, hears, or understands another and connects with the other, acknowledging that level of knowing. Intimacy is not simply empathy. It is empathy with connection. Intimate moments do not necessarily make intimate relationships. An intimate relationship is one in which intimate moments are shared over time, with a spoken or unspoken agreement or commitment to witness the experience of the other in an ongoing way. From the checkout counter to the football game, from the carpool pick-up to the dinner party, our daily lives are filled with intimate moments.

One of the word games I like to play is to come up with a new "Intimacy Type" every time I have an experience with someone in which there is a shared sense of knowing, seeing, and understanding. I find that naming that newfound connection not only raises its value but also increases my positive feelings throughout the day.

Like the "Financial Intimacy" I have with my accountant and the "Concern-For-My-Child Intimacy" I have with David's teacher at school. Like the "Neighborhood Intimacy" I have with Hank and the "Humor Intimacy" I have with Arie, who sends me just the right jokes by e-mail. There's also the "Musical Intimacy" I have with the people at the summer folk festival and the "Gastronomical

Intimacy" I have with the man at the potluck, the one who seeks me out to get my hummus recipe.

And it gets even deeper than that. There's the "Professional Intimacy" I feel with my colleagues, the ones who really get it about my most brilliant work—and I about theirs. And there's the "Religious Intimacy" I feel with others during times of elevated ritual. There's also the Fatherly, Motherly, Sisterly, and Brotherly Intimacy I feel when I am with my family of origin or the people who have become my family of choice.

There are those even deeper levels of intimacy: the "Conversational Intimacy" I have with my girlfriends and a hand-ful of guyfriends as we listen and respond to the events in each others' lives; the "Interpersonal Processing Intimacy," where we strive to understand our part in the struggles we are having with others; and the deepest "Intrapersonal Processing Intimacy" I have with very few others, where we witness each other's vulnerabilities and emotional wrestling as we deal with our own shadows.

There are no specific time criteria associated with these inti-macies. Some of the people with whom I share these intimacies I check in with on a daily basis. Others of them I touch base with only once a year. Some of the intimate moments, like the one with the woman in the grocery store, are with people whose names I'll never know. The frequency and personal level of connection are not what lie at the heart of intimacy. Rather, the distinguishing factor of any intimate moment is that when it's there, it opens up your heart and you can feel it in your gut.*

---

* Go to unexpectedintimacy.com for tips on building intimate connections.

Gastronomical Intimacy

*My idea of heaven is a great big baked potato
and someone to share it with.*

~ Oprah Winfrey, talk show host,
philanthropist, actress, publisher

THE SHARING OF FOOD IS FERTILE GROUND for intimate experiences. The sensuality of textures and the excitement of flavors have deep connections to our earliest experiences of pleasure and intimacy. It all starts with milk. In my case, it was specifically sweetened condensed milk.

For years, every time I ate certain foods, I would have this vague "back to the womb" feeling. Comfort food, some call it. For me it is vanilla pudding, *dulce de leche* ice cream, and any caramel-type foods. It wasn't until I was vacationing in Jamaica fifteen years ago that all the pieces fell into place.

My Ex Jack and I (married at the time) were staying at Teng Sing Pen, a small gathering of huts by the beach in Negril. Every morning, there would be fresh mango and papaya, Blue Mountain coffee, toast, and sweetened condensed milk. The milk was so thick you could spread it on the toast, and it made the coffee taste like nectar from the gods.

It also took me right back to the womb. One morning, as I was having a little toast with my sweetened condensed milk, it hit me. My grandmother, "Nanny," was a great cook and a magnificent baker. Born in 1900 in Lithuania, she came from the old school and didn't know a lick about low fat or diet alternatives. I learned to make scrambled eggs from Nanny—the secret was to mix a little cream in with the eggs. She died when I was ten and was debilitated for a few years prior to that. As a result, I don't have too many strong memories of her cooking, but I know she used sweetened condensed milk—and a lot of it. Hence, I concluded that when I was little, she probably fed it to me. When I got back from Jamaica, I shared my insight with my father. I suggested that maybe Nanny gave me sweetened condensed milk when I was a baby and that's why I have this back-to-the-womb experience with that particular flavor/texture. No, he said, it wasn't Nanny; it was him.

Tears filled my eyes. I could just picture it. I was a little baby, probably an infant, and my father was holding my little body in his big, warm arms. Maybe I was distressed or perhaps he just wanted to share a little sweetness—the same sweetness his mother shared with him—with his little girl. He'd dip his pinky into the can of thick, sweet milk and then slide that gooey little finger in my mouth. Yum!

Today, in our (darn it!) health-conscious times, I would not have dreamed of giving sweetened condensed milk to my infant, but now that he is older ... now I share *dulce de leche* ice cream with David and the flavor takes me right back to the womb. I tell him the story about Jamaica and about my Nanny, and then he asks about when he was a baby. That leads to us taking out the photo album and looking at pictures—of him as a baby, of me as a youngster, of my father as a young man, and of my Nanny. The gastronomical intimacy of four generations connecting through the taste of sweet milk is reincarnated within those pages.

Of course, gastronomical intimacy goes beyond the bonds of blood relations. Between the years 1977 and 1986, I traveled to Israel seven times and spent a total of almost two years of my life there. Much of that time I spent in and around the Old City of Jerusalem. My intimacy with the land is a whole other story, but right now, I want to talk about a sweet treat that was responsible for not only many intimate moments but also even some long-term friendships.

During every trip I took to the Old City, I had my gastronomical routine. On my way into the Arab quarter, I would stop at one of the shops and have a cup of mint tea with one the shop owners. That is one of the most civilized customs, isn't it? Don't do any business until you've had a cup of freshly infused, very sweet mint tea.

After the tea, I would go to Abu Shukri's (located in front of the fifth station of the cross on Via Dolorosa) to eat hummus with pine nuts and to drink the sweetest fresh-squeezed orange juice you've ever tasted. The shop was run by two brothers, who had inherited the restaurant from their father. To this day, his picture still hangs on the wall.

After that scrumptious meal, I would weave my way through the narrow cobblestone street to one of the sweet shops. There, next to all the flaky, nutty, honey-drenched sweets like *bakláwah* (*baklaváh* if you eat Greek) was something called "*kanafi*."

Kanafi—imagine a very large tin lid, four feet in diameter, with a lip two inches high. The proprietor first sprinkles the lid with oil and some kind of orange dust. Then he lays down a layer of cooked, shredded wheat, something like *couscous*, only not seasoned. Next, he spreads out a half-inch layer of goat cheese. All the while, a flame blazes under the lid that is slowly heating the entire circle. The icing on the cake, as it were, is a hot, sweet, thin syrup that is ladled on top of the whole concoction just before it's divided and served.

The ambiance around the sweet shop and the serving of the *kanafi* was an experience all its own. The small shop was filled almost exclusively with men. Just outside, the atmosphere burst with the hustle and bustle of the Old City—beasts of burden carrying sacks of grains and boxes of merchandise, young boys carrying large portable tea dispensers on their backs, people haggling over prices. It was especially wild to be there on a Friday, following the afternoon prayers, when the mosques let out. People would swarm into the sweet shops and pay their two shekels for a plate of *kanafi*. If you were lucky enough to arrive when the heating/layering/melting process was well under way, you didn't have to wait too long. Finally, when the *kanafi* was done to the satisfaction of the proprietor, he would begin to divide and conquer. A quick three spatula chops and a flip, and orange wheat crust becomes the top, with the melting cheese and syrup underneath.

Now, your mouth might not be watering, but the description of the food has almost no connection to the experience of eating it. All I can tell you is that the combination of the warm soft cheese with the sweet syrup and slightly crunchy crust would make you blush.

And it's not just me. Over the course of those ten years, I shared the "*kanafi* experience" with dozens of people. After meeting and eating at Abu Shukri's, I would take them by the hand and lead them to the sweet shop, Jafar and Sons. Skeptical, always, based on the description of the food, some were reluctant to try it. I would, however, urge them and they would acquiesce. Plate in hand, we would find a table and, together, take the first bite.

At first, their hand would hesitate as they lifted the fork to their mouth. The first taste lands on their tongue. Next, their eyes would tilt slightly to the side, trying to identify the flavors. And then, just before swallowing, it would happen. Their face would flush as the flavors erupted in their mouth and they struggled to keep the soft, warm, sweet nectar from sliding down their throat, wanting the sensations to remain longer on the taste buds. Then our eyes met with that knowing ... a fabulous moment of gastronomical intimacy.

One of the friends I took for the *kanafi* experience was Caroline. She and I had met as volunteers on a moshav (cooperative village) halfway between Jerusalem and Tel Aviv. I remember taking her on a Tuesday, and then on Wednesday bumping in to her in the Old City. She had an as-of-yet-unknowing friend in tow, on their way for the *kanafi* experience. We gave each other a knowing wink as we bid farewell.

More recently, in Boulder, Colorado, I went to lunch with Eve. I had just completed the religious ceremony of divorce (her husband was the officiating rabbi) and she offered to take me to lunch at the local all-you-can-eat Indian buffet down the street. Interesting new dishes always seem to grace the serving tables at these buffets. Me, well, I'll try anything, so when the curried cabbage entree appeared, I figured what the heck and took a sample. Eve is a vegetarian, so while there are always choices at the buffet, they are somewhat limited. She took a generous portion of the cabbage.

Eve and I were having an intimate conversation. Her mother had passed away recently and she was describing to me her journey through the grieving process. She talked about having gone through the anger, through tending to end-of-life logistical details, and then finally really being able to grieve that her mother was gone. As she told me all this, she cried. I cried with her. We were sharing real, raw emotions. After a bit of respectful silence, I told her about the writing I was doing and how I was loving my new single life. As I spoke, she was engaged and present with my story. I felt heard and witnessed. But the intimate moment I remember best was just after my first mouthful of the curried cabbage. It was incredibly delicious. The flavors and crunch and warmth were so unexpected from cabbage that I stopped mid-sentence and exclaimed in a somewhat whispered voice, "This is delicious!" The corners of Eve's mouth went up into a sly smile as our eyes met, and she said, "I know."

On the other hand, just as powerful as gastronomical intimacy can be in long-term friendships, the inability to share gastronomical intimacy can be a red flag in the search for that "let's share our lives" kind of intimacy. I had a first date with a smart, handsome man I had met online. He invited me to breakfast and asked me to pick the restaurant. After some deliberation—first impressions and all that—I chose what was, at that time, one of my very favorites: Panera's. Panera's is a bakery and beyond. The menu consists of soups and sandwiches and salads, each one tastier than the last. My current favorite was a "You pick two" with a bowl of thick and savory roasted garlic and portabella mushroom bisque, Fuji apple chicken salad with pecans and gorgonzola, and a piece of fresh-out-of-the-oven French baguette. There is also a wide array of tempting bakery items such as scones and danishes, savory egg soufflés, and sweet sticky buns. And if that weren't enough, the decor is delightful, complete with a gas fireplace and wireless Internet. That's not to mention that the coffee is only $1.50 a cup with free refills.

My date, Alan (not his real name), told me he had never been to a Panera's. "Ooh!" I thought, "a virginal experience. What a treat it will be to share the textures and tastes and allow the ambiance to inspire this new relationship." I wondered if he would *ooh!* and *aahh!* over the soups and salads or just head for the sweet pleasures.

Well, things don't always turn out the way you hope they will. Alan arrived and said he'd eaten a bowl of cereal earlier that morning and that he wasn't that hungry. He didn't even look at the menu and just got himself a cup of coffee. He said he didn't usually go to these "Einstein Bagel/Starbucks" kinds of places. He didn't get it, and it was over before it had begun.

So while Alan and I didn't see each again, Caroline and I, twenty-five years later and 1,500 miles apart, are still friends. It just goes to show the power and pitfalls of Gastronomical Intimacy.

Hajimete — First-Time Intimacy

Would that you had come yesterday,
then God would have let us be friends longer.

~ Hamid, Rashida Tribesman, Ethiopia,
Meeting someone for the first time

SEVERAL YEARS AGO, I SPENT SEVEN MONTHS living in a small city in Japan. There, with a culture that in so many ways was 180 degrees different from my own, every day I was exposed to new angles and filters for everything in life I had taken for granted—bathing, eating, greeting, discerning what to say, understanding what not to say, knowing how to handle incurring and repaying obligations. Every day I was pushed to consider, "Why do I think/do this?" I am sure I learned more in those seven months about myself, and the framework in which I exist, than people learn in years of therapy. In the bank of life experiences, it was one of the richest deposits I've made.

What an intimate culture and language the Japanese have. On the surface, it may not seem so. People talk to each other on the subway, sitting next to each other, with their faces straight ahead so they look like they are talking to themselves. It is considered somewhat offensive to look each other in the eye. People rarely invite others into their homes. Their public spaces are where they meet and their private space is just that: private.

But there is a deep underlying understanding of the emotional life that is expressed in the Japanese culture. For example, when someone gets a little drunk and gets up to sing karaoke, it is understood that the person is relieving some stress in his/her life. It is accepted without judgment. The language too, has layers of understanding. For example, there is a word, *sumimasen*, which is used as a kind of light "thank you," but the form of the word is in the negative. It literally means, "I can never repay you." It might be used if, let's say you are walking along the street and the wind blows your hat off and a stranger picks it up for you. The sense of obligation is so strong in the culture that you owe that person for that favor, and at the same time, you recognize that you will not be able to repay the debt. There is another telling word: When someone has a new experience, they say, "*Hajimete*," meaning "I am knowing this for the first time."

During my brief seven months in that Asian nation, I made daily use of the word *hajimete*. I had a job teaching English as a second language in a kind of adult social club. Although for the first two months I didn't see another non-Japanese person, when I finally did meet a few, I learned that the question was not "What are doing?" but rather "Where are you teaching?"

Where I was teaching was American Plaza. It was one of a dozen "English Social Clubs" that were scattered throughout the country. Membership to the club was sold through *Encyclopedia Britannica* salespeople. I was the only teacher in this club and I was also technically the office manager, although truth be told, with my scant knowledge of the Japanese language, the Japanese secretary (the only other employee) did all the managing.

There were officially 200 members at the Okayama branch of American Plaza. The deal was that they joined for two years and were entitled to attend 100 classes, an average of one each week. Soon after they joined, I needed to administer a "level test" to place them in the right class. I would speak to them for a few minutes, but in reality, I could determine their level after about thirty seconds.

Here's how the test would go: First, I'd say hello. Sometimes the students, with sweat pouring down their faces, would simply stare at me with a frightened look. These people I put in "Intro 1." Classes with those students would be the most basic, primarily helping them to get over their fears of speaking English. There were other students who were enthusiastic but had no clue about how to speak. To my hello they would immediately answer "Herrow!" and I would move on to the next question, "How are you?" These students would enthusiastically respond with the same "How are you!" and I knew they were "Intro 2" material. If they got past the "How are you?" part of the test with an answer of "Fine" or "Fine, thank you," I would move on to the final question.

"I see you live in Okayama," I'd say. And then very slowly I would ask, "Were you b o r n in Okayama?" Well, this last question really separated the men from the boys. Those who sort of understood but didn't exactly know how to answer went into "Beginner" and those who understood and could answer went into "Intermediate." Out of the 200 students, I had six intermediates, twenty beginners, and the rest Intro 1 and 2. I had no advanced students. Needless to say, for seven months, I s p o k e v e r y s l o w l y.

Every single day I was enjoying new experiences—new food experiences like eating *natto*, a gooey fermented soybean glob that I did ultimately acquire a taste for; new cultural experiences like understanding the Japanese currency of obligation and conformity in a group; an appreciation for what it feels like to be an alien—a *gaijin*—the ultimate outsider.

My students were also engaging in new experiences with me such as crossing a street at night when the light was red and learning curse words in English. For many of my students, I was the first *gaijin* they had ever spoken with. And Jewish person?—well, that's a whole other story.

I very quickly learned to use "*Hajimete!*" What an intimate expression! With that one word, you let everyone know that this experience is new and you are excited, and maybe a little scared, and definitely a little vulnerable. You say "*Hajimete!*" and everyone around you goes into small, quick nods of acknowledgment. "*Hajimete, hajimete*" everyone murmurs in a deep, instant intimate acknowledgment of witnessing your virginal experience. Those who have known it before have the vicarious pleasure of experiencing it again as if for the first time.

We all have plenty of new experiences and see others in that state. We don't always think of it as intimate, but if we take the time witness it, intimate it is. It could be as simple as hearing a new piece of music or more profound, like how Jack felt at our son's birth as he cut the umbilical cord. It can be an individual moment, or as when Neil Armstrong walked on the moon, a national moment. We have those experiences and we are intimately connected to other people who are going through those same experiences. It is *Hajimete!* Intimacy.

Hajimete Meets Jewish Women

We seek not rest but transformation.
We are dancing through each other as doorways.

~ Marge Piercy, poet, novelist, social activist

IN 1991, I MOVED TO FORT COLLINS, COLORADO. At that time, the city was nearly unknown to anyone outside the state. In Denver, they referred to it as a cow town. In reality, it was a city whose growth curve was about to explode. Within the first couple of years of our residence there, Fort Collins was rated by three top-ranking magazines as the best place to live and the best place to retire. Sonny Lubick came to town as the football coach for CSU. Barnes and Noble moved in. Whole Foods opened. The highway signs in Denver that had, up until then, indicated Laramie, Wyoming, as the point north on I-25 were replaced with signs to Fort Collins. Cow town no more.

We moved to Fort Collins for Jack's work. He had gotten a job as the rabbi/cantor for the only synagogue in town. At the time, there were 85 families that had joined as members, although word had it that there were a lot more Jewish families living in Fort Collins who had not affiliated themselves with the synagogue. The synagogue itself was not affiliated with any particular Jewish denomination. I used to like to say that there was the whole range there, from A to Z—Assimilated to Zealous, although surely more of the former than the latter. Let's face it, people didn't move to Fort Collins as part of their Jewish path.

Many of the congregants had come to Fort Collins in the 1970s. Most of them hailed from New York or other large cities on the East Coast. One couple told us their unlikely story—they were on their way to California from New York and ran out money in Fort Collins. Eventually they both became psychologists and are now in private practice. Other people had come to teach at Colorado State University, in the English department and in the prestigious school of veterinary medicine. Still others came, very specifically, to get away from anything that reminded them of the middle-class Jewish suburban experience of their youth.

And what brought them into the synagogue? For some, it went something like this: They had children and when their children turned seven or eight or nine, they would have sleepovers at friends' houses. Sometimes on Sunday morning after the sleepovers, they would go to church with their friends. Sometimes they would hear things in church like "The Jews killed Jesus." They would then come home saying, "Mommy, Sally told me that she learned that the Jews killed Jesus. We're Jewish, aren't we, Mommy?" Quickly, Mom would open the phone book to see if there was a synagogue in town. Hopefully, she would pick the number for Har Shalom rather than the other synagogue (Messianic-Jews for Jesus type) listed. She would then come in to check it out.

But that was before Jack hit the scene. Soon Jack, whose previous career was a folk-rock singer/songwriter and recording artist, was singing with the Baptists, offering words of celebration and prayer at citywide events, and meeting with leaders and community members on a regular basis. Being the charismatic guy that he is, he had his picture in the paper almost every other week. By the end of the first year, everyone knew there was a synagogue in town.

I also did my part. One month after our arrival, I advertised the first "Woman's *Rosh Hodesh*" (New Moon) gathering. According to Jewish tradition, *Rosh Hodesh* was given as a women's holiday in recognition that they didn't participate in the Golden Calf "incident" at Sinai when Moses was gone getting the Ten Commandments. Evidently, the men all gave their jewelry to make an idol. The woman didn't. Hormonally speaking, legend has it that if we were still rising with the sun and sleeping with the moon, not living with all the artificial lights that fake our systems out, that all women would menstruate at basically the same time, with the New Moon. The New Moon is a special time for women to be together as Anita Diamant described in her bestseller *The Red Tent.*

The celebration of *Rosh Hodesh* by Jewish women is a recently renewed tradition. It is really only in the last thirty years that we have seen small groups of women come together with the new moon. In Fort Collins, up until 1991, it was virtually unheard of. Forty women showed up at the first gathering.

Each month, for the next ten years, we met every month, on or near the new moon. At some of our gatherings, we looked at traditional text, like the story of Adam and Eve, from the perspective of Eve. Turns out, Eve wasn't kicked out of the Garden—only Adam was. So we asked ourselves questions like "What went on for Eve that she ultimately left the Garden? Did Adam beg her to come with him or did she ask to go? Did she have to think about it—what her life would be in the Garden and what she imagined it might be outside the Garden? How did she process that? Did she speak with the plants and animals? With the angels?" If the gathering were large, we'd break into small groups for a discussion. If it were small enough, we would sit in a circle and share all together. In all cases, the text would come alive for us.

Other months, we would study a contemporary text, such as Judith Plaskow's *Standing Again at Sinai* where, after looking carefully at the language in the text, she poses the provocative question: "Were we (the women) there (at Sinai)?" Still other months, we would look at our lives as text. Using a "fishbowl experience"—people with a common link sitting on the inside with the rest of us, holding a container on the outside—we might choose the topic of "Motherhood." Inside might first be women who are mothers, followed by women who are not but wanted to be, then women who are single mothers, women who feel like single mothers, and women who are struggling in relationship with their own mothers. Those of us not choosing to be inside would sit in a circle surrounding the women on the interior. We were the womb and were there to hold the energy—to witness the experience of those on the inside. An emotional discussion would inevitably ensue.

Each month, we'd frame the whole experience as a ritual. We'd begin with lighting a candle. We'd bless the space with a sense of gratitude for arriving at this moment. We'd set an intention for the evening that was related to the theme. We'd go around the circle and check in. We'd study and discuss and witness. We'd close with a song and a prayer. During one gathering, we created a sacred box—a wicker basket that held our prayers, ritual objects, books, and notes from previous meetings. Every woman contributed her mark. Each month, someone became the Keeper of the Box.

Every year at Passover, we would have a Women's Passover *Seder** on the seventh night—the night they say the Hebrew people crossed the Red Sea on their way out of Egypt and into the Sinai wilderness. We would partake in the *seder* together, approaching the ritual from a feminist perspective. Forty days later, we would hold the pinnacle event of the year: Our annual June retreat. Twenty-five of us would go away together—three days on a dude ranch in Wyoming—where we would have more than just an evening together. We wrote our own interpretations of the prayers and led our own services. We studied, laughed, sang, danced, and hiked together.

One year, we invited a crone from our community, Marvelle K. Marvelle is an artist and a lover of life, and I affectionately call her Razzle Dazzle. She led us through a mask-making process— two hours of silence while we all slathered our faces with Vaseline and applied layer after layer of medical plaster patches (casting material). What would emerge was a very personal expression of who each of us was. We embellished the images with paints and glitter and fabric and gems. We danced with our masks under a canopy held by our sisters as we proclaimed our intentions for ourselves for the year. There was "Fork in the Road Woman" and "Feeling Six Woman." There was "Be Here Now Woman" and

---

* *Seder* means order and is a long, involved meal with 14 parts that happens during Passover. Traditionally, it is done on the first night. Some people also do a seder on the second night. Special interest groups have been known to add yet another.

"Embracing the Sacred Woman." I was "Letting Go Woman" on more than one occasion.

The truth is that there were so many levels of intimacy going on between and among the *Rosh Hodesh* women that I had a hard time giving it just one name. In the end, the "first-timeness" overshadowed the rest. It was the first time that the women of the community had come together in a powerful way. It was the first time most of these women had explored Jewish texts. It was the first time these women had taken their place in Jewish ritual. It was the first time for many of them that they had connected with Spirit in a Jewish context. For many, it was the first time they had felt meaning in their lives as Jewish women.

I recently returned to Fort Collins. "Embracing the Sacred Woman" had made a surprise 50th birthday party for her husband. Among the seventy-five-plus people in attendance were a handful of women who had been in those first years of *Rosh Hodesh*. We stood together in a circle and were overcome by the intimate feelings we still possessed for one another. Time could pass and distance could separate us, but in some powerful and intimate way, our hearts were—and would always be—tied together.

Waterfalls

Wind moving through the grass so that the grass quivers.
This moves me with an emotion I don't even understand.

~ Katherine Mansfield, writer

IF YOU ARE LOOKING FOR *HAJIMETE* INTIMACY, you could book a ticket to Japan or seek out a peak religious experience, or you could head to the nearest preschool or playground. It seems like young children have a *hajimete* experience every seven seconds. That number doesn't come from any well-funded study and it might be a little exaggerated, but young people do have *hajimete* moments more than any other group I can think of.

I recall a profound *hajimete* experience with my son, David. When David was two years old, his godmother, Dodi, and I took him to Lory State Park, which was twenty minutes outside of where we lived in Fort Collins, Colorado. Lory State Park is a prime example of Colorado open space—with boulders and pine trees and where hogbacks that are older than the mountains jut up through the earth, reminiscent of the time when the Rocky Mountains erupted. There are a number of self-guided trails in the park. My favorite is Well's Gulch, a three-mile loop that passes through seven eco-zones as it moves up and around the foothills.

Well's Gulch seemed a little daunting with a two-year-old, so we decided on the quarter-mile trail out to the little waterfalls. David, in his usual way, talked the whole way from the parking lot, through the bushes, over the rocks, right until we arrived at the waterfalls. The moment we arrived, something quite out of the ordinary happened. David got silent.

First, you need to understand that David loves to talk. He's been a yacker since he said his first word ("hat") at twelve months of age. At sixteen months, when he'd wake up in the morning, he'd call out to me to get him from his crib. After nursing a little, he'd look up at me and say, "Let's talk."

Up until that moment at the waterfalls, David had never really experienced the power of nature, the sound and sight of rushing water, the feel of a cold mountain stream. Never mind that it was a mini-falls. Totally and completely mesmerized, David was having his virginal waterfall experience.

I tried talking to him. "Isn't this wonderful? Do you like the waterfalls?" He didn't hear me. Dodi tried too. "David," she said, "look at these beautiful stones!" No response. It was as if he were paralyzed. Gently, I handed him a small, smooth river rock and showed him that he could throw it into the pool of water that was collecting at the bottom of the falls. He made no eye contact, but as an indication that he had heard me, he bent down to pick up a river rock and tossed it into the water. Then he picked up another, and another. At some point, I took off his shoes and socks so he could feel the sand and water on his toes. Later, I showed him how to draw with a stick in the little sandy area at the edge of the pool.

Dodi and I eventually sat down on some large stones and laid out the snacks we had carried in with us to have a picnic. David didn't eat. He was alternately throwing stones, dipping his toes, and drawing in the sand. A full forty-five minutes passed and David had not said a word. Such prolonged silence had never happened before, and it hasn't happened since. For me and for Dodi, it was a witnessing of a pure *hajimete* moment.

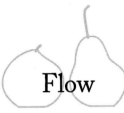

Flow

This is happiness:
To be dissolved into something completely great.

~ Willa Cather, author

B Y SOME MEASURE, THE ULTIMATE INTIMACY IS
Union. It is a central concept in Buddhism and Taoism, and
it can be seen in the Zen practices such as Aikido, Kendo,
and Ikebana. In the Jewish tradition, it is spoken of as *devakut*:
cleaving to God. In 1990, Mihaly Czikszentmihalyi (pronounced
chick-SENT-me-high) wrote a book called *Flow* that articulated
this sense of union with everyday life. Czikszentmihalyi's concept
of flow is the mental state of a person who is fully immersed in
what he or she is doing. It manifests with feelings of energized
focus, full involvement, and often is accompanied by success in
the process or the activity. It is an in-the-moment intimacy with
the moment itself.

This type of relationship—being in the zone—is often ascribed
to athletes and artists. But Czikszentmihalyi, a scholar and one
of the founders of the emerging discipline of Positive Psychology,
believes this flow can be experienced by everyday, ordinary people.
In fact, he has spent decades studying how people all over the
world experience flow, in work and in play.

Indeed, in my younger, more athletic days, I felt this flow while
playing tennis. The racquet felt like an extension of my arm and
as it received the life force of my opponent through the medium
of the ball, this feeling of flow coursed through me. Then, as the
ball absorbed my life force and I directed it to my opponent's weak
spot, I felt its pulsation yet again. In this way, the energy on the
court became one organism. In my more recent days as an organi-

zational artist, I've felt this flow as, for example, conference planning unfolded. From that first flash of a vision of the entire event, and then with facility as my canvas and my faculty program proposals as my palette, the vision of the whole radiated through me. Feeling its power, I began a process of shifting the hues and creating sparks, muting some parts while illuminating others. Although it entailed thousands of details, each one was so connected to the whole that the experience was of Oneness.

On an even more mundane level, I can reflect on my relationship with maps. Being a visual—spatial-type person, I have always related to cartography. When I was young, my parents did a lot of traveling and my father was into maps. Before each trip, he would hang one on a wall, using it as a building block in his trip-planning efforts. As I got older, I took on the practice. In fact, a ten-year period (from 1977 to 1987) unfurled, during which I was traveling, spending more time outside the United States than in it, when maps became one of my best friends.

My relationship with maps and directions might even qualify me as a Master Wayfinder. In fact, I used to run workshops called "Which Way Do I Go?" They were designed for people (mostly women) who have trouble with directions and get lost easily. When I look at a map, I become one with the geography. I place myself in a virtual "You are here" spot and then am able to find my way anywhere. I have traveled all over the world and have never gotten lost. I must have that aura around me because I often have people, strangers, ask me for directions, even in a foreign place. Funny thing is I can usually help them. When I first got my driver's license, I used to head in a new direction and try to get lost. Inevitably, I would come across a large cross street that I knew and could position myself on the map in my mind.

You could even show me a map of Tokyo, point out the subway station and the post office, and then, in reality, plop me down at that subway station. Without a hitch (or a map), I could find my way straight to the post office's doorstep. What's so astounding about this feat of mine? Well, the directional savvy I possess would be difficult for some to conceive of, even with the map, given that in Japan many streets have no names, and those that do are written in Japanese characters. Something, however, happens to me when I read a map. Like Alice tumbling down the rabbit hole, I am transported into the design. In every pore, I can feel the twists and turns that are needed to get from Point A to Point B. Like a homing pigeon, I can lock the destination in place until I find a way to reach there. In perfect union with each other, the map and I become One.

Intimacy, Our Immune Systems and the Brain

There is magic in the memory of schoolboy friendships;
it softens the heart, and even affects the nervous system
of those who have no heart.

~ Benjamin Disraeli,
British statesman and literary figure

IN THE PAST TEN YEARS, WE HAVE SEEN AN explosion of research about the human brain. The subject of the chemicals in the brain as they relate to love and relationships has appeared on the cover of nearly every major magazine. What we are learning is that the neurophysiology of our brains (i.e., how our neurotransmitters send and receive messages to produce and release hormones) is directly related to the quality of our relationships. In other words, who we relate to and how we relate with them significantly influence the way our brain develops. It turns out that when we feel connected, it stimulates all kinds of good flowing of our hormones and neurophysiology. It also bolsters our immune system. It can even determine our moods. Recent research claims that our relationships may even determine the life force of our bodies.

The opposite is also true. In his best-selling book *Social Intelligence*, Daniel Goleman reports that love seemingly can make a medical difference. Among men getting angiography as part of treatment for coronary heart disease, those whose loved ones were reportedly least supportive had about 40 percent more blockage than those who reported having the warmest connections.*

Robert Putnam, author of *Bowling Alone*, goes further when he reports how the data indicates that "People who are socially disconnected are between two and five times more likely to die from all causes."

Goleman makes a biological case for "becoming more intentional about our interpersonal world." He reports that "vibrant social connections boost our good moods and limit our negative ones, suppressing cortisol and enhancing immune function under stress ... that the lonelier a person feels, the poorer immune and cardiovascular function tends to be ... and that as we age, neurogenesis, the brain's daily manufacture of new neurons, slows—likely from monotony." He continues, hopefully, that bringing intentionality to our relationships may contribute to keeping our brains young and flexible.

What this means is that we have way more power than we thought we had. If we can think about our relationships in a positive and healthy way, we can boost our immune systems. And perception is powerful—this tendency likely holds true for all kinds of relationships, even those virtual relationships we have with celebrities and fictional characters. Now, of course, no one is advocating that your intimacy constellation be made up of virtual, and fictitious relationships—humans need physical closeness, touch, eye contact and real time relationships—but energetically speaking, if we value the role each relationship plays in our own personal constellation, we can create around ourselves a nurturing energy field of health, happiness, and satisfaction.

---

* Men who reported feeling loved most strongly had the very lowest levels of coronary artery disease. While having a loving mate offers protection, being trapped in a toxic relationship may be harmful to your health. See T.E. Seeman and S.L. Syme, "Social Networks and Coronary Heart Disease: A Comparative Analysis of Network Structural and Support Characteristics," Psychosomatic Medicine 49 (1987) pp.341-54.

The Wissahickon

*The clearest way into the universe
is through a forest wilderness.*

~ John Muir, preservationist,
writer and philosopher

ONE OF THE BIG DIFFERENCES BETWEEN THE
Rocky Mountains and the East Coast is the amount
of water. Colorado is considered semi-arid—that's
the technical word for really dry—while the coastal region sees
plenty of rainfall. This morning, as I was rubbing bees wax hand
cream onto my dry, chapped hands, the humidity was nineteen percent. Each year, the first snowfall in the mountains is
something to celebrate, as the snow pack is our main source of
reservoir water. While there are trees, the native ones are mostly
pine with an occasional cottonwood popping up where there is
a trickle of water nearby or underground. The mountains really
are rock (hence the name Rocky Mountains), with some pines
and aspens growing at the lower elevations and not much nourished at the top. Of course, the other side of the coin is that we
have 300 days of sunshine. We also get to see the 14,000-foot
almost-year-round snow-capped peaks of the awesome Rocky
Mountains as a backdrop to our lives.

Compare that with the mid-Atlantic around Philadelphia. In
Philadelphia, you really get four seasons. Winters are thirty-three
degrees and slushy, and summers are rainy, hot, and humid—the
kind of days where ten minutes after your morning shower, you
want to shower again. In the middle of winter and the middle of
summer, you wonder, "Why …?"

But the payoff comes in those vernal and autumnal seasons. Just
when you think you can't bear another mid-Atlantic winter day,

springtime arrives in all its glory. The floral colors blaze—azaleas, magnolias, rhododendron, dogwood, cherry blossoms … flowering bushes they've never heard of in Colorado*. Life bursts from the earth, and every few feet a different kind of plant pushes forth with its unique life experience in relation to the sky and the sun and the other plants around it. The large oaks and maples spread their branches as a canopy over the streets. Take a walk or even drive down the street and you are gently held in Mother Nature's palm.

David and I go to Philadelphia every year for Thanksgiving. While we are living in Colorado, the rest of my family of origin remains in Philadelphia—my parents, sisters, cousins, aunts, uncles …. I try to get back there two or three times a year, especially as my parents age into their eighties. If I'm lucky, it's been a late autumn and I get to luxuriate in the last vestiges of fall colors.

Autumn is something else altogether. If you've never been to Philadelphia (or New England) in autumn, you ought to put it on your "Things To Do Before I Die" list. It's my favorite season just about anywhere in the Northern Hemisphere, and in Philadelphia, it is nothing less than spectacular. And if you do go to Philadelphia, you ought to take a walk in the Wissahickon.

The Wissahickon is part of the Philadelphia park system. Benjamin Franklin, an incredibly far-sighted visionary from Revolutionary times, consecrated 9,200 acres of land within the city of Philadelphia as parkland in perpetuity. In fact, "Fairmount Park" is the largest park within a city in the entire country. The Wissahickon is part of that system.

So it was a Sunday on my last visit to Philadelphia and I walked in the Wissahickon for hours. The combination of the oranges, yellows, and reds in contrast with the green grass and blue skies is part of my vision of heaven. Add in a swiftly flowing creek, a gravel pedestrian/horse path and an occasional old covered bridge and you start to get a picture of the Wissahickon. I walked so long and deep into the trees that I no longer felt like an intruder but rather

---

* Did you know that every March, Philadelphia houses the largest indoor flower show in the world? The Philadelphia Horticultural Society has been hosting the Philadelphia Flower Show for 175 years and it is not to be believed.

one more specimen of organic life in the forest. It was a beautiful day on the edge of the end of autumn. The air was fresh and the creek was flowing. I could feel the trees letting go of their leaves. Wanting to capture the essence of the moment, I stopped and stood still. The air pulsed against my skin. I could see the trees talking to each other. I used to go there and practice Tai Chi among the trees. If you are still enough, you can hear them breathe.

Sound of Music

Music is well said to be the speech of angels.

~ Thomas Carlyle, Scottish essayist,
satirist, and historian

WHEN IT COMES TO INCITING THE SOUL,
nothing quite measures up to music. How is it that
something so intangible and ethereal as vibrations
in the air can stir such emotion? I can trace my past through the
sentiments conjured up when I hear particular pieces of music:
Carol King and "Tapestry" during those hormone-charged days
of summer camp; Joni Mitchell and "Miles of Aisles" which
Micky and I played a hundred times on our first parent-free
road trip to Canada; Mike Oldfield's hypnotic "Tubular Bells"
in the college dorm; and Peter Mayer while condo-camping at
the Lyons Folk Festival—3,000 people in a beautiful field by the
river, kids inner-tubing on the free-flowing water, no smoking,
feel-good culture, great music, and exotic international cuisine.
These are just some of the images that are recreated in my mind
whenever a life-defining melody reenters my eardrums.

No doubt about it, the mystery of music speaks to our soul. It
is so powerful, in fact, that it can even cause us to fall in love.

The first time I met Jack, I was living in Philadelphia. It was
the fall of 1989 and we were both at a weekend retreat for the
Jewish holiday of *Simchat Torah*—a celebration of receiving the Ten
Commandments at Sinai. Since my niece was in a Jewish preschool,
which was closed for the holiday, I did my sister a favor and brought
along my young relative for the long weekend. I loved having her
with me, so much so that I was introducing myself to everyone as
"Leah's Aunt." Jack remembers meeting "Leah's Aunt," but I was

pretty consumed by that role and didn't really notice him.

The next time I saw him was a few months later when I was working on a new business—a (pre-Internet) mail-order catalog of Jewish stuff. I needed some input on what music to carry in the catalog and someone said, "Do you know Jack? I don't know the guy, but he says he knows about music. Maybe you should ask him." I did and he was enthusiastic and helpful, but I didn't think anything more.

The third time I saw Jack was a few months later. Although he was living in New York, he was coming to Philadelphia every couple of weeks to study with his teacher, Reb Zalman. He needed a place to stay when he was in town. After speaking with my room-mate, Julie, we offered him a place with us. That arrangement settled into a routine where he'd come every few weeks and stay for a couple of days. He was a singer/songwriter and his music would fill the apartment whenever he arrived. He had songs for kids, songs for grown-ups, songs for *Shabbos* (the Sabbath), eclectic styles of folk, rock, reggae, and the haunting minor-key melodies of Hassidic Jews. He got a place to stay and in return we enjoyed his company. It was kindness, nothing more.

Then a little twist poked its way in. Julie was a single mom. She had one child and wanted more, but she didn't have a man in her life with whom she could make a family. She was looking for a donor. She had already asked a couple of other guys who, after seri-ous deliberation, had said no. Too much psychic responsibility, they said. After a couple of Jack's visits, I suggested she consider asking him. He seemed like a nice enough guy, I reasoned. Heeding the suggestion, Julie asked him and he said yes. He said that he could see what a great mom she was with her first child and that he would be honored. It seemed such a very generous and selfless act. I took notice, but at that point, it was about Julie and making a baby, not about me, and I didn't feel anything stirring.

A few weeks later, during one of Jack's visits, he asked if I wanted to hear a new song he had written. It was a version of *Ma Tovu*—a song that is sung near the beginning of every morning service and is probably one of the first Hebrew songs every child learns. It consists of six words that are repeated a few times, sometimes sung in a round. The six words get translated as "How goodly are your tents, O Jacob, your dwelling places, O Israel" and comes from Numbers 24:5. In that Biblical passage, the prophet Balaam is sent to curse the Israelites, but when he arrives, he is overcome with awe by the life the Israelites have made for themselves. Instead of cursing them, what comes out of his mouth is a blessing.

As with many Hebrew songs and prayers, many people don't really know what they are saying or why they are saying it. And even if they do, after a while it is done by rote, without much thought to what they are actually saying. At that point in my life, my Jewish connection and learning was all about fighting that tendency and finding the deeper meaning in each prayer, song, ritual, and action. It is called *kavanah*—Intention.

So there on that day, on the porch of the house that served as a gathering place for community and worship, Jack sang to me what he had written. He used a traditional melody for the six Hebrew words—*Ma tovu ohalekha Ya'akov, mishk'notekha Yisra'el*, but then he added verses in English that brought the story alive.

He sang:

His name was Balaam
and he came to curse us
but when he actually met us
he was blown away
by the quality of our home life
and how we did worship
our Unseeable God
our Impalpable God
our Source Universe God
he had to say

(chorus)
Ma tovu
ohalekha Ya'akov,
mishk'notekha Yisra'el

How wonderful
is your home life, Ya'acov
and your worship places, Yisrael

The words cut deep and the music carried me away. I was transported to the desert, where I could feel myself both among the tents of Jacob and on the hilltop with Balaam, overlooking the community. Like the roots of a tree know the earth, I could feel the heat and slower pace of life, the tension between the discouragement of wandering and the hopefulness of a new life. I could feel the paradigm shifting as idol worshipping was giving way to the idea of Oneness. And in that moment, we were blessed. *That's* why we sing *Ma Tovu*, that's the *kavanah*! I felt a chill as the hair on my arms stood up. The boundaries between prayer and music and musician blurred, and I fell in love.

Babies

It was the tiniest thing I ever decided
to put my whole life into.

~ Terri Guillemets

WHEN I WAS IN MY LATE TEENS AND TWENTIES, I spent more time traveling outside the United States than I spent here in America. Four different times I set out from "home" with a one-way ticket, a landing place for the first few months, and wide-open plans after that. I had my traveling routine that became my home away from home—three items that I kept on my person: my lima-bean-shaped purse that I wore under my shirt and in which I carried my passport and traveler's cheques; a extra large, tan, plastic teacup that I got at Shirley's breakfast hut in Skowhegan, Maine; and a good book. I had, in my backpack, three changes of clothes and fourteen pairs of underwear (putting off the need to do laundry for as long as possible). I had the thinnest bath towel you can imagine that I had picked up in Finland, and Dr. Bronner's soap, which could be used for clothes, utensils, and brushing one's teeth.

I had amassed a collection of "little things"—a miniature deck of cards, a teeny chess game, a set of two-inch knife, fork, and spoon, and matchbook-size dictionaries. It was the late 1970s so there were not yet CDs, let alone iPods. I had a Sony "Walk About," a cousin of the Walkman that was a combination tape player, stereo recorder, and radio.

I went all over the world armed only with those minimal belongings. In countries where it was really expensive to live, I found work. In countries where one could live on a few dollars a day, I just hung out. In countries where the living was more middle class, I studied and got college credit (and got my parents to subsidize it!). In almost every case, my reason for returning to America was that I had run out of money. The exception was in 1984.

My sister Lisa, although the middle daughter, was the first to get married. She was also the first to get pregnant. In October of 1984 she was expecting her first child. I had spent the year leading up to that time traveling—seven months working in Japan, a month traveling in China, and three months volunteering on a kibbutz in Israel. I wasn't out of money—I had made quite a bit teaching English in Japan. I wasn't out of ideas of where to go next—Turkey was and still is on my list. But for the first time in my life, I was homesick. It was the anticipation of the birth of the first in the next generation of my family that pulled me home.

I arrived back at my parents' house about two weeks before the due date. Every day, I checked in with my sister about how she was doing. As the due date drew closer, she was, as is natural, getting more and more tired of being pregnant. The narrow creek in front of her house was overhung with a small bridge that was cracked, making it a very bumpy crossing. She and her husband would crash over it a dozen times a day, hoping to bounce the little one out into the world.

Finally the day came—Oct. 8, 1984—and Leah was born after many hours of labor. For the first twenty-four hours, my exhausted sister could barely keep her eyes open. As a result, I was the first one to hold the baby. She spent that whole first day either in my arms or by my side.

For the next few months, I didn't have a lot going on. My expenses were very low (living at my folks' house) and I still had some money left over from Japan. So, for the time being, I was a woman of leisure. Playing with my niece Leah was an almost every-day event. As the years passed, the geographical chasm between us eventually grew wider. She is now twenty-two and a full-grown woman. We do not talk regularly and I mostly hear about her through my sister. But when I do see her, or even think about her, a smile erupts from somewhere deep inside.

Here's what I believe: that from the time babies are born, until they are about six months old, they are not very shielded. I believe their soul stuff is not yet solidified for this human journey and that the boundary between them and everything they interact with is more fluid at that time than it is at any other point in the human journey. For this reason, I think it is really important during their first six months to pay special attention to the kind of stimulation infants get.

On the other hand, I think that those of us who are lucky enough to be included in the circle of these little ones' first few months partake in a mystical experience. I believe we bond and attach at a "soul cellular" level in a way that lasts forever.

Other than with Leah and my own son, I have had that kind of relationship with two other babies. One is more recent—she only just turned three. The other, Rosi, is much older. She is just finishing her freshman year at college.

I lived with Rosi for the first eighteen months of her life, often playing with her and rocking her to sleep. Shortly after that, I moved out to Colorado. Over the years I have seen her erratically. I don't really know a whole lot about her life nor she about mine. But the bond between us is so strong that whenever we do see each other, even now that she is nineteen, all she wants to do is crawl into my lap and all I want to do is hold her.

Caretaking

*The most basic and powerful way to connect to another
person is to listen. Just listen. Perhaps the most important
thing we ever give each other is our attention....
A loving silence often has far more power to heal
and to connect than the most well-intentioned words.*

~ Rachel Naomi Remen, clinical professor,
medical reformer and author

I GOT THE CALL AT 6:00 A.M. TAMARA (not her real
name), my old contemplative martial arts instructor, was on
the edge. The previous night she had discovered that her husband had been having an affair. He was a high-level executive, was
well respected in his field, and traveled a lot. He was out of town,
and she was home alone. She called because she didn't know what
to do and was reaching out for help.

Prior to her desperate phone call, I was already in a role of helping Tamara. Really, we were helping each other. She was writing an
autobiography and I was coaching her and helping her to edit it.
In exchange, I was getting lessons from her. I have always been an
alpha female type and have spent most of my life working on my
own projects. As a student, I had served as class president on more
than one occasion, as a young adult I traveled on my own around
the world, and as a income-earning adult, I have almost always had
my own business. So this supporting was a stretch for me, and I
welcomed the experience.

On the exterior, Tamara had the appearance of a strong and
secure woman. She had studied many years with a master and, as
far as I was concerned, was a master in her own right. She told me a
story once about how there was an intruder in her home and while
still in her bathrobe, she grabbed the martial arts sword. With a
growl, she came darting toward the intruder, weapon brandished.

One look at the sword and the crazy woman in her bathrobe and the guy was outta there.

On this particular day, however, Tamara was not feeling so strong. When she called at six o'clock in the morning, she haltingly outlined the facts of her situation and then added that her brother suffers from schizophrenia and that she was afraid that she might fall off that cliff. She had called her closest friend, but her friend couldn't get there until about 10:00 A.M. Could I just sit with her until then?

So there I was in Tamara's foyer, where I found her in a daze. I went into the kitchen and made some tea and we sat in the living room in silence. At one point I said, "Tamara, you look so tired. Why don't you lie down?" "Yes," she answered and stretched out on the sofa, but her eyes remained wide open. At that moment, I had an impulse. I removed the big cushions from the back of the sofa and lay down behind her. I put my arm around her arms and chest and we just lay there. After a few minutes, she turned her head toward me and said, "Bless you."

What a powerful intimate moment. Whether from aging, stroke, accident, grieving, or other trauma, sometimes people are truly vulnerable, unable to care for themselves. The caretaker becomes vulnerable too, but in other ways—Will I say the right thing, offer the right support? Tuning in and simply being present until there is a knowing of what is needed to take care—that's what is required.

Peacemaking

An enemy is someone,
whose story we haven't heard.

~ Gene Knudsen Hoffman,
International Peacemaker

EVERYDAY I THANK MY LUCKY STARS THAT I WAS born an optimist. Rarely do I feel the emotion of hopelessness. I have a creative and resourceful mind that generates—often too quickly—a myriad of solutions to any problem. There is, however, one situation that takes me to that dark place of hopelessness: When I experience, either directly or as an observer, the severing of a relationship as a response to conflict.

Let me clarify this. I am not saying that there are not times when the getting the heck outta there is appropriate. When there is abuse, or the situation is chronically violent, then removing oneself from that environment is not only appropriate but it is necessary.

Barring that extreme situation, there are so many ways to respond to conflict. Severing of communication is but one. Making war is another. Neither of those choices are very productive ones. I prefer talking and listening. As the wise-woman Phyllis Berman wrote in her interpretive rendition of King David's Psalm 30, "You have taught me that death of relationship comes from *not* saying, not from *saying.*"

Fortunately, I have had very few personal experiences where someone has refused to talk with me as a response to conflict. And I don't recall any situation—with one exception—where I shut down to the possibility of reconciliation. That one exception was not with a person, per se, but rather with a situation: The conflict in the Middle East.

Between the years of 1977 and 1985, I visited Israel seven times.

Cumulatively, it was more than two years of my life. My feelings of intimacy deepened as I got to know the land and the people. My emotional connection with everything Israel was intense. There was a time when I could not imagine myself living anywhere else.

During my first trip, Anwar Sadat, then president of Egypt, spoke at the Knesset—the first Arab leader to do so. It was a time of hope. Then in 1982, Israel invaded Lebanon. Israel invaded—that had never happened before. It changed everything. First it was disbelief and then it was anger. And then it happened, I felt hopelessness descend.

I spent years in that place.

What that looked like was that I didn't read any news about the Middle East and when conversations would start around the dinner table, I would excuse myself to go to the Ladies Room. All my creative problem solving skills meant nothing—the problem had no solution.

Then, a few years ago, I stumbled upon an organization called Seeking Common Ground. Luck would have it, it just happened to be in Colorado. Seeking Common Ground runs a program every summer where they bring teenage girls together—Jewish Israeli, Palestinian and American young women—for two weeks of communication skill building, leadership development, and dialogue.

One Palestinian participant wrote about how she pushed through conflict: "I found myself in a corner with a Jewish girl called Moriya. We started to talk about the Palestinian-Israeli conflict and every word became difficult. Throughout this challenging argument we mentioned "freedom fighters." We chose this issue to discuss because I was with the freedom fighters and she couldn't believe it. She was simply in shock.

When Moriya started to talk about feelings, I felt pain like a person being stabbed with a knife. It's true that I made her cry and hurt her when I told her that I agree with the freedom fighters, but she was the only person that made me cry because of what I've said.

After we finished arguing, I went out from the room for

maybe 10 minutes. I smelled the fresh air of the mountains, heard the whispering of the birds, and saw the beautiful blue sky, and I realized that there is still hope. As Moriya changed my perspective maybe I can change what Moriya thinks about the Palestinians.

The next day I went to apologize to her because our friendship means a lot to me. If I really think deep in my heart, I would say that the argument with this special girl and the program, itself, changed so much in me. The experience made me a better person in society. I am a person who can now handle pressure and stay open-minded to the other side's beliefs. It was an experience that I can't forget because it truly made a difference in my life."

Another participant wrote, "...When I first met the Israelis I thought of them as an enemy and I was afraid to ask why I think that way, but during the program I dared to ask why, and found no answer beside that it was our societies and history books that taught us to be enemies. By the end of the program, I discovered that the society is not always a good teacher, and books are not wiser than the human heart."

My hope was restored.

And, my discovery of Seeking Common Ground opened up a whole world of communicative reconciliation. For example, The Compassionate Listening Project, which teaches "skills used to heal polarization, cultivate healthy relationships, and build bridges between people, communities and nations in conflict." Compassionate Listening, they go on to say, "focuses on strengthening the influence of the heart through cultivating compassion, and learning to listen and speak from the heart, even in the heat of conflict."

One of the early participants in The Compassionate Listening Project was Rabbi Andrea Cohen-Kiener. She wrote the following poem, inspired by a dialogue she had with a Palestinian man about his son—she and he both living in the United States, both of them with strong feelings about the Palestinian-Israeli conflict. It is reprinted here with her permission.

Because...

Because I love these hills, this landscape, these deer and
rivers and vines —
    I understand why you do.
Because I need to feel at home in this place —
    I understand why you do.
Because the life stories of my people bring me here, hold
me here,
    I understand that yours do.
Because I remembered this place and felt attached to it
even when I wasn't here —
    I understand that you did too.
Because the vagaries of history have convinced me that I
need to be here, with secure borders and a national
identity —
    I understand that you do too.
Because — when I have felt afraid of you — I have imag-
ined that you are a murderous beast, somehow inhuman,
    I understand that you have imagined me this way too.
Because my fear has brought me to act in ways that
were powerful but immoral and cruel,
    I understand that yours has done so too.
Because I have felt alone, abandoned by the world's nations,
    I understand the additional burden of feeling alone in
    your suffering.
Because my ancestors are buried in these hills,
    I understand why the graves of your people are a sacred
    magnet for you.
Because I want to move freely in my land and grow and
raise my children and my tomatoes and my spirit in
freedom and health in this place,
    I know that you need this too.
My need does not cancel yours.
My need helps me know yours.

Yes, it does, Andrea. Thanks for helping us remember that.

Guys and Intimacy

*I feel closest to my (guy)friends when I do something
with them—working toward a product or sharing a goal.*

~ Drew Paryzer, playwright

THE FIRST FEW YEARS I LIVED IN FORT COLLINS,
I taught in the synagogue's Hebrew School. Each year, a
group of us would travel to Denver to attend a regional
workshop for Hebrew school teachers. This particular year, there
were seven of us and we decided to make the ninety-minute drive
together. Lorie took us in her van.

I was all the way in the back, sitting next to Herb. Herb was my
contemporary and, after a couple of years of therapy, was what you
could call psychologically evolved. We got into reflecting on the ups
and downs of our lives and relationships and, in fact, spent the whole
ninety minutes on the subject. Herb revealed himself to me and I
to him, as we honestly and openly processed some of the harder
issues in our lives. As we pulled into Denver, Lorie called back to us,
"What have you two been yacking about?" Simultaneously I said,
"Relationships" while Herb, winking at me, said "Sports."

A few months later, I found myself at a community event,
standing between Herb and Andrew. Andrew was another guy I
knew who was also psychologically reflective and with whom I also
had had deep Conversational Intimacy. I introduced one to the
other and said, "Hey, you guys should know each other. You both
know how to have deep conversations." They looked at each other
then back at me, and then both scrunched up their noses and in
unison said, "Naa!"

In that moment, I realized that guys can be girlfriends to the
gals but not as easily with other guys. Intimacy between guys, it
seems, is a whole other ball game.

Nothing-Is-Taboo Intimacy

If you can't be direct, why be?

~ Lily Tomlin, actress, comedian,
writer and producer

(All names in this section, except Felice Yeskel's,* have been changed.)

CONVERSATIONS ABOUT PERSONAL FINANCES are rare outside the accountant's office. Fears of scarcity, jealousy, and the notion of just plain old taboo keep people from sharing financial intimacies with others.

Of course, there are the accountants and financial planners. They are the individuals with whom Financial Intimacy traditionally takes place. These professionals know how much you make, how much you spend, and how much you owe the bank. If they are good, they can give you some advice for tax savings and can help you plan for college and retirement.

In 1987, I had an experience that completely altered my relationship with money and opened up a whole new world of Financial Intimacy. I was part of a group of thirty-six women who began meeting over Memorial Day weekend every year. We called ourselves *"Achiyot Or"*—Sisters of Light. The basic idea was that it was a safe time and space to explore radical Jewish feminist thought and practice with other like-minded women.

Although I believe we were all politically left of center and we were definitely all women, the homogeneity ended there. Some women were married; others were single. There were lesbians and straight women in our midst and others who identified some-

---

* (Executive Director, Class Action, www.classism.org, a national nonprofit working to end classism)

where in between. Some women had children; some did not. Some had money; others did not. Some were rabbis; some were otherwise Jewishly educated; still others were not. Most were Jewish, but some were not. Age-wise, there were women in their twenties through women in their sixties. All were ready for some new experiences, to be engaged and challenged in their thinking and practice.

"Radical" is a relative word. It can be radical to go to college if you are the first in your family to do so. It can be radical to be a teacher if your father and his father and his father before him were all lawyers. It can be radical to study for a test if all your buddies have decided to blow it off.

In this case, radical meant that we were pushing the envelope in the Jewish and feminist realms. Like the *Rosh Hodesh* group, we explored what the Jewish texts and prayers really mean for women. The space at our retreat was defined as "Lesbian Space, open to all women"—a direct challenge for those of us who didn't define ourselves as lesbians to experience what it felt like to be accepted, but just on the margins.

My strongest experience at *Achiyot Or* was the year Felice Yeskel and her partner Barb introduced us to the concept of "cost sharing."

In advance, Felice had gotten us all to agree to spend a good deal of time over the long weekend to engage in this process. We knew the weekend was going to cost a total of about $7,000. How we would, as individuals and as a group, decide to pay the total fees was to be determined. There were two or three women in the group who had so much money that they could have written a check for $7,000 and it would not have impacted the quality of their lives at all. There were other women who were unemployed and had accumulated personal credit card debt and for whom any amount was going to be a stretch.

During the three-days, we went through a number of processes to help us see, feel, hear, and understand our relationship with money in a way we had never done before. We learned how our relationship with money is both objective—we have actual, measurable dollar amounts of assets and liabilities and income and expenses—and subjective—we have feelings about the amount of money we have.

We witnessed the experience of others as they gained insights into their own relationship with money. Like the "fish bowl" exercise, those women who identified themselves as working-class individuals came into the middle of the circle and spoke about that experience. At first, there were five or six women who ventured in, but slowly, after the discussion in the bowl progressed, a few more women entered. I remember Karen was crying as she came in. Although up to that moment, she had been identifying herself as from the upper class (her family had come from Europe, before the Holocaust, where they had been wealthy), she was remembering that when she was a little girl, her mother had received food stamps and that the upper-class status was just an illusion.

We explored how our economic class and experience from our family of origin shaped our relationship with money, regardless of our current economic situation. For example, Barb shared with us a story ....

She and her friend were social activists. They didn't earn much from the work they did, but it was tremendously satisfying. They had just finished a project and were both beginning to look for work. Barb noticed that she and her friend approached the job search in completely different ways. Her friend, who was raised in a working-class family, was scouring the Want Ads in the newspaper, looking for a job that would pay the bills. Barb, although currently in the same working class as her friend, was raised in an upper-class family. Her approach was different. She was thinking, "What organization do I want to work with, what job title do I want, who do I know that might be able to help me, and how can I write my resume so I will get an interview?" Unlike her working-class friend, she had a sense of entitlement. We were learning about classism and learning about each other.

Next, we formed into small groups based on our current type of work. Then, we went into other small groups on the basis of what we thought we should contribute to the weekend. After more discussions in those groups, we wrote down on a piece of paper a pledge—how much money we thought we ought to contribute.

Then we did the most radical thing. Something, according to some, that was quite taboo. We disclosed an accounting of our assets and liabilities, our income, and a general budget for how we spend our money. We put that information, along with our tentative pledge toward the cost of the weekend, in a pile. Then we each looked over each other's financial lives: real estate, stock, bonds, and checking accounts; student loans, credit cards, and car payments. Net worth, personal debt, money spent on therapy, and hair coloring. It was all there, exposed. I remember Dana crying during that process, very aware how outraged and disapproving her parents would have been by such personal disclosure.

And we didn't stop there. Armed with objective financial data, we challenged each other about our pledges. I told Marcy that I thought she was contributing too much. She was taking on more than her share given the level of credit card debt she had. Maybe that's why she had the debt? She was spending beyond her means, not making appropriate choices in her consumption. But wouldn't people think she wasn't doing her part if she pledged less, she asked. She didn't want people to think that about her. We talked some more. Yes, it was feeling a little out of control, and yes, she could use some support to get back on track.

I also challenged Jill. Her net worth totaled in the millions. She was in the category of those attendees who could write a check for the whole shebang and not have it impact her quality of life. The question I wrestled with was what amount was right? Should she wait to make a pledge until after everyone else had and then just pay what was left? Should she take the average cost of about $200 ($7000 divided by evenly the 35 women) and double it? Triple it? How does someone with that level of financial resources at her disposal act in a way that is helpful, respectful, and appropriate and not in a way that is patronizing or rescuing?

That experience forever changed my relationship not only with money but also with other people and their money. I am not particularly impressed by net worth, either large or small. I am equally comfortable sitting in a room with multimillionaires as I am with people who are struggling to get by. I know plenty of people with large resources who have plenty of troubles, and I wouldn't change places with them "for all the money in the world." I also know lots of people who, objectively, have less but are satisfied with their lot in life. I am much more impressed by the choices people make in their use of the resources they have than the actual tally of their bank account.

Now, a personal transformation wasn't the only thing that transpired from this economic sharing experiment. This Financial Intimacy experience also changed my relationship with the women who shared it with me. One of those women, Nadia, has recently moved to Denver. Although it had been nearly 20 years since we shared that weekend together, we discovered an instant reconnection. I find myself calling her when I have to think through the implications of financial entanglements. I know that she will be able to set her own "stuff" about money aside and help me process what is going on both objectively and subjectively.

What's more, one kind of intimacy has led to another. The last time I saw Nadia, I found myself uncomfortable with what I felt was a disrespectful manner in which her daughter treated her. In most cases, I would think to myself, "It's none of my business." Parenting style—another taboo subject. But given our Nothing-Is-Taboo Intimacy, I spoke to her about it. She has thanked me a number of times since then, and based on our conversation, she and her daughter have started their own deep conversation about the roles of parents and children and the nature of respect.

Breaking taboos is a bold move and can be a little scary. It's a little like getting naked and is not appropriate for every relationship. Often times I have found myself staring into the eyes of a silent and unknowing conversational companion, realizing that our current topic has been shut down by something taboo. But more times, when I reveal something about myself, I find my companion immediately relax, and with a certain kind of permission, s/he is able to bring her/himself more fully, intimately in relationship with me.

The Mint Room

*Nothing can beat the smell of dew and flowers and the odor
that comes out of the earth as the sun goes down.*

~ Ethel Waters, blues vocalist and actress

THE MINT ROOM AT CELESTIAL SEASONINGS in Boulder, Colorado—those of you who haven't been there are probably thinking, "The Mint Room? What is she talking about?" But what you have to know is that those of us who have been there are all having an intimate moment, right now, thinking "Oh My God, The Mint Room!"

The tour of the Celestial Seasonings headquarters begins in the front lobby, where we find an array of Dixie-cup-sized samples of a half dozen teas. Sometimes there is a new infusion, one that's in the market research stage, and we are invited to give our opinion. The tour winds its way through the marketing department, where full-size versions of the beautiful artwork and the pithy aphorisms that are found on the Celestial Seasonings boxes of tea line the corridor walls. We hear the history of how Mo Siegel started the company picking herbs from the mountainside outside of Boulder in 1969. We see photos of the communities all over the world where the herbs and spices are now grown and harvested.

The next stop is the factory floor, where we gaze upon space-age robots mixing huge vats of herbs, measuring them into teabag quantities (eight million bags a day) and assembling and sealing the boxes into cases. The last stop before the gift shop is the warehouse, where all the herbs are stored. There are boxes stacked from floor to thirty-foot ceiling, each one stamped with its contents and country of origin. All of the garage-like rooms are open but one. "The Mint Room," we are told, "must be kept closed because the smell is so intense that it would permeate all the other boxes and compromise the integrity of the other tea." The tour guide tells us that she is going to open the door for a minute for anyone who would like to go in.

The garage door opens just enough for us to duck and move into the space. It looks just like all the other spaces, with bags of herbs stacked floor to ceiling, and for a very brief moment, we are all thinking, "What's the big deal?" And then it hits us like a tidal wave. First the eyes, which don't know whether to open wider or shut completely. Whichever we choose doesn't matter—there is no stopping them from watering. Next it hits the nose, and a brief moment later, the lungs. It's like Vicks Vaporub on steroids as we all feel sinuses clearing and bronchial tubes opening.

Many of our comrades have already fled the experience and then the real challenge begins—who is going to stay in there the longest. I think it's going to be me, as I inhale even more deeply. "Refreshing" doesn't even begin to describe the experience as the cells on the skin of my exposed arms and face begin to tingle. Time stands still as I imagine myself skinny-dipping, jumping into a cold, clear spring-fed lake in Maine, on a chilly morning, every pore screaming, "Oh no, yes!" The experience is so neurally pleasurable, it's almost orgasmic. Unfortunately, that makes it too enticing for words. I guess you just hadda be there.

Literary/Dramatic Intimacy

When I only begin to read, I forget I'm on this world.
It lifts me on wings with high thoughts.

~ Anzia Yezierska, novelist

MY FRIEND NAOMI FROM THE REDWOODS and I share *Star Trek* Character Intimacy. She stayed with us recently and I was telling her which two episodes of *Star Trek Next Generation* had touched me most deeply. We were walking at the time and when I said the titles of my favorites, she dramatically stopped walking, gasped, and clutched her heart. Yes, those were her most memorable episodes, too.

Star Trek gives us a great example of TV Character Intimacy. Captain Picard and Commander Riker are so real for us that we can begin to predict how certain events will make them feel. Do you remember the bumper stickers during the 2000 presidential campaign that read "Picard/Riker 2000"? Those of us who knew these characters really felt that they were the kind of leaders that would be good for our country. Because of their outstanding qualities—who they were and how they handled life—we wished for them to be real. (See page 167 for more on *Star Trek* Intimacy.)

Books, movies, and live theater, too can convey that intimate experience. One of my favorite ways to spend a Saturday is to curl up on the sofa with a great book. Although I read a lot of nonfiction, there is nothing like a great story—one where I am swept away into the lives of the characters, feel that I know them, and care what happens to them.

Authors of fiction will tell you that they have an intimate experience of writing their stories. The characters take on lives of their own. I've heard more than one author say things like "I was hoping she (a character) wouldn't do that, but she did."

Novels and films aren't the only genres that can create this virtual intimacy. Movies, too, can bring on this feeling of intimacy. Take, for example, the movie *Crash*, which is about racism and how everyone makes assumptions about "others," mostly out of frustration about their own lives. As viewers, we are immediately drawn into the lives of all the players—Black, White, Iranian, Latino, Korean. Some are rich and some are poor; some are cops and some are criminals. The acting is terrific and the story is engaging, so much so that we find ourselves feeling for each character and caring what happens to them.

There is a scene early on in the film where a white cop, played by Matt Dillon, pulls over what he thinks is a mixed-race couple (corporate executive black husband, light-skinned black wife). He proceeds to molest the woman as he does a body "search" while the husband looks helplessly and vulnerably on. We later see the ripples of this act as Dillon's partner asks to be reassigned and as the couple experiences increased tension in their relationship.

Toward the end of the movie, there are three and a half minutes—that's 210 seconds—of the most deeply intimate moments of the film.

The first sixty seconds — The Setting

The bad-boy white cop and his new riding partner come upon a traffic jam. They get out of the car and we can see that there is an accident ahead. One car has some flames coming out from under its hood and another car is flipped upside down on the road ahead. Dillion calls to his partner, "Call it in …" as he jogs and then runs to the site of the overturned car. He tries the door but can't get it open. He keeps glancing between the car in flames fifty yards away and the gas dripping from this overturned car, and the tension builds. He stoops down and we see that there is a bleeding woman strapped into the car. He calls in, "Ma'am, can you hear me? Are you hurt?" We hear her answer through quiet sobs: "I can't breathe." She is hurt, bleeding, and disoriented, and her seatbelt is nearly strangling her. Dillon's partner yells over that the fire trucks will be there in two minutes. Dillon yells back to get the extinguisher and put that fire out. Gas dripping, tension building. "I'm gonna get you out," says Dillion as he moves in toward the victim, through the broken window.

The second sixty seconds — The Freak-Out

The woman turns her face and we see that it is the light-skinned black woman whom Dillion had humiliated the previous day. Her face is inches from his and when she recognizes him, she starts to freak out. "No, no, get away from me, not you, stay away from me." We feel her anger and her aversion to having anything to do with her molester. Despite her protests, Dillon is still trying to undo her seatbelt to get her out. Screaming now, "Don't touch me, not you, anyone else, not you …"

"I'm trying to help," Dillon whines while struggling with the belt latch. Frantic, now, she cries, "No, no, get your filthy f___ing hands off me! Don't touch me. No, No No!!!" We understand that there is a part of this woman that would rather die than be touched by this seedy cop again.

Finally, Dillon yells, "Lady, I'm not going to hurt you!" They are both silent. A look—is it regret?—passes across Dillon's face. More quietly he says, "I'm not going to hurt you…. That's gas dripping and no one else is here yet and I need to get you out." We see the woman look at the gas and the fire ahead. For the first time, she realizes her predicament.

The next sixty seconds — The Work

"I need to reach across your lap to release your seatbelt. May I do that, please?" Dillon asks with cautious respect. As he squirms to get beneath the woman, their foreheads touch. She nods slightly. Her dress is bunched up at her hip, and as his hand passes by her leg, he tugs on her dress to cover her exposed thigh. "Are you really going to get me out?" she asks with a hint of hope and disbelief that this is happening. "Look at me," he says. Their eyes meet. "I'm going to get you out." Their noses are almost touching and she is crying, her tears dropping onto his face as he struggles beneath her to undo the seatbelt. It won't release.

"I have to cut the belt," he says as he flips open a knife. "Oh my God!," she cries. "Everything's going to be fine, Everything's going to be fine — Look at me, I'm going to get you out," he assures her.

We see a river of gas flow under the car ahead and catch on fire. The flames quickly spread back toward the pair's car. There is a mini-explosion and lots of smoke and the car, with both of them in it, is in flames. At that moment, the backups have arrived and they are tugging on Dillion to get him out. He loses his grip on the woman and she is stuck inside—the smoke and flames billowing around her. Dillon scrambles back in to get a good hold on her and yells, "Pull!" to his partners.

The final thirty seconds — The Safe Escape
Dillon pulls the woman free, out of the car, out of harm's way. He has her in his arms as the car, now behind them, explodes for real. The woman is clinging to him. He wraps her in a blanket, cradles her head, and holds her as she sobs into his chest. The medics are there, and for a moment, she looks up at her rescuer and does not want to let go. At that moment, they are, ironically, intimately one.

As she is walking away, with the support of the medics, toward the ambulance, she turns her head and looks back at Dillon and the two minutes that transformed them both. She shakes her head ever so slightly at the irony. We glimpse Dillon's face and see that he is also feeling—we hope that it is a sense of shame and regret for the sh_t he has been in many of the relationships in his life. We imagine that as a result of this intimate experience, he will mend his ways.

Literary and Dramatic Intimacy don't have to be heavy to be intimate. David brought home his own poetry book—a wonderful project in which the kids wrote poems, fine-tuned them, and then illustrated their own poetry in a pre-bound hardback book suitable for a home library. What a wonderful memory from second grade. I read David's poetry and I loved it! He really used some wonderful imagery and brought me deeper into relationship with both his subject matter and his own experience of that subject matter. I especially loved the one called "Goldfish."

Goldfish
like tiny
poppable orange whales
swimming, swimming
in the
dark
deep
dangerous
sharkful blue sea

I called my mother. I read her the whole book, cover to cover. Her favorite was "Snow." She loved how David really caught the emotion.

Snow
like white sun
falling,
falling
run,
run,
run

Be it a favorite novel, movie or poem, we can experience moments of intimacy with characters, events, and places that are real only in the realm of our minds. Yet the power of the mind being what it is, these moments can stimulate our feelings of empathy and connection, influence actions we take with real people, and ripple into our everyday lives.

Family

*Call it a clan, call it a network, call it a tribe, call it a family:
Whatever you call it, whoever you are, you need one.*

~ Jane Howard, novelist

Commitment

*Commitment is inherent in any genuinely loving
relationship. Anyone who is truly concerned for the
spiritual growth of another knows, consciously or
instinctively, that he or she can significantly foster
that growth only through a relationship of constancy.*

~ M. Scott Peck, psychiatrist and author

WHEN I START THE CONVERSATION ABOUT
"all these different kinds of intimacy," I sometimes
encounter happily married people who get a little
defensive. "Hey, wait a minute," they say. "What I have with my
spouse is very special. It feels like you're not valuing that relationship."

On the contrary.

Many of the types of intimacy described in this book are what
I call "The More The Merrier" type intimacies. Hey, I'd be happy
to have an intimate cheesecake moment or share the thrill of riding the rapids with just about anyone. When it comes to a small
subset of intimate relationships, however, they are reserved for a
select few.

Up until now, I've mostly been writing more about intimate
moments than intimate relationships. While I do believe that in
every intimate moment there lives a seed for an intimate relationship, a moment does not make the relationship intimate.
Commitment is what makes a relationship intimate.

Everyone has her or his own list of "one and only," private,
reserved categories of intimate relationships. My list includes (but
is not limited to) my son, my family of origin, my family of choice,
and my family of circumstance. For many people, the list expands
to include clergy, doctors, financial advisors, handymen, and hair
stylists. Any relationship you have that you consider "exclusive"—

in which there is only one person or group who fits the category, and indeed that category is sometimes named for them—has a very special value. There is a sense of commitment and loyalty about it. The relationship also tends to evolve over a period of time. In most cases, you've weathered some ups and downs and together you've decided that the value of the relationship is worth seeing it through. Sometimes, those that have gone through some "severe weather" transform from one kind of intimate relationship into another. The quality that sets them apart is a two-fold commitment: to strive to be a knowing witness and to allow oneself to be knowingly witnessed.

In this book, I haven't included too many stories about my family of origin—my parents and my sisters—not because the relationships among us are not intimate, but rather because it is *expected* that those relationships are intimate. We expect to have relationships—for better or worse—with our blood relations. Despite a lot of childhood sibling tension (understatement) and parental fumbling, I'm happy to report that at this point in the journey, we all like each other. However, I live in Colorado, 1500 miles away from my blood family. In our mobile society, the concept of family must extend beyond blood to include those individuals with whom we surround ourselves every day. It is those non-blood individuals to whom we open our eyes, open our arms, and open the circle that are the focus of this book. In addition to growing healthy connections with our family of origin, we need to learn how to recognize and cultivate both our family of choice and our family of circumstance.

Making Families

*Nobody has ever before asked the nuclear family to live all
by itself in a box the way we do. With no relatives,
no support, we've put it in an impossible situation.*

~ Margaret Mead, cultural anthropologist

IN THE STATE OF COLORADO, SINCE 1999, WHEN
A husband and wife who have children file for divorce, they
are obligated, by law, to take a "Parenting After Divorce"
class. I applaud the state for this level of consciousness. I think
of all those other groups of people who would benefit from such
focused attention. I've often imagined this mandatory example
turning into a series of law-enforced classes for grown-ups such as
"Marrying Before the Brain Is Completely Developed (under the
age of twenty-six)" and "Parenting through Menopause [Staying
Cool When the Hot Flashes Strike]."

The class I took when I found myself in the "divorced with
child" situation was surprisingly direct and focused. There were
fifty or sixty participants and two therapist/facilitators. Both
facilitators were parents after divorce themselves, and they engaged
us with sociological statistics, entertaining role-plays, and great
advice. They normalized the experiences people have and they
validated the wide range of feelings divorcing families experience.
Their main point throughout the class was that the quality of the
relationship between parents directly impacts the amount of scar-
ring on the children. They noted that this tendency holds true
whether parents divorce or not. Good point. Makes sense.

There was only one moment in the day when, from my perspective, the facilitators blew it. Toward the end of the class, Harry
(not his real name) asked, "How many people here come from
families where the parents divorced?" About half the room raised

their hands. Then he said something like "Let's do our work so we break that cycle."

I found myself shocked. Up until that moment, Harry had been open minded and accepting, validating, and normalizing, supportive and wise. But in that statement, he made one HUGE assumption. He incorrectly concluded that, when children are involved, long-term monogamy is what is right and that anything other than that is wrong and needs to be fixed.

I beg to differ.

There is much anecdotal evidence to support the contrary. If permanent monogamy with procreation were really the normal, "right" way for humans to mate, like say the way it is for mallard ducks, then like mallard ducks, we would *all* be doing it—and doing it successfully. Obviously, that is just not the case.

The notion of choice is the thing that makes humans unique in the animal world. Some humans are strict vegetarians and some are avid meat eaters. Some humans prefer to live in small apartments on the twelfth floor in downtown Manhattan where the shower is in the kitchen and the density of humans is high; others prefer to live close to the earth in the country where the nearest neighbor is miles away. When we study the life of bears, we don't find that some eat only berries and others only chickens. When we look at owls, we don't see that some like to sleep at night while others are more "day-owls." Unlike other animals, we choose where we want to live and what we want to eat, and we don't necessarily follow the mold. This uniqueness, I believe, extends to the choices humans make about making families.

In the landmark Scientific American book written in 1989 called *Sexual Selection*, authors James Gould and Carol Grant Gould look at mating and procreation behaviors in all life forms we know of—beginning with how bacteria and viruses "do it" and including plants, fish, reptiles, birds, and mammals. Within the book's pages, the authors describe so many different ways life and family manifest in our world that I was humbled. It is one thing to see ourselves in our own little self-centered, human-centered world, emotionally responding to the daily satisfactions and annoyances of our particular journeys. It is quite another to see ourselves in the context of all life across all time. *Sexual Selection* contains a wonderful, eye-opening, perspective and is surprisingly readable for the lay person.

Although procreation among bacteria may be interesting, I focused my time more on those forms of life that are slightly closer to ours. It turns out that there are very few species that, as a rule, mate monogamously or for life. The Goulds identify six basic social systems among animals. The significant factors that differentiate the various species and lifestyles have to do mostly with how long the males stick around after copulation and how invested they are in their children.

Only one of the six basic lifestyles is "monogamy," with one male and one female. Within monogamy, the Goulds further identify three sorts: permanent, annual, and serial monogamy. They go on to relate that they have found that the motivations for entering into a monogamous relationship differ between males and females. Interesting ...

Just as humans span the whole range from vegetarian to carnivore and city dweller to home-on-the-range, I'm thinking they also span the range—or at least have a variety of impulses—when it comes to making families.

Let's assume for a moment that this thought is true, that we each might have natural impulses and orientations that are not aligned with the permanent nest-type monogamy. Each of us has our own orientation and might be more like moose or wolves or lions. Wouldn't it be interesting, then, if by exploring some of the animals' ways, we could better understand some of our own needs and choices? Just for fun, I tried to envision five lifestyles, as described by the Goulds, from the human perspective.

Tending Bonds of the Moose

Moose (males and females) are solitary during the year. In the spring, they come together for days or weeks of mating. The guy fends off his competition, and the one who wins gets the girls and then goes off afterwards to look for another female. Meanwhile, mom hangs out to rear the kid for months. The male-to-male contest is strong. The female impassively watches and waits and then acquiesces to the winner. The female motives for submission to the victor are not clear—is it natural selection to go with the stronger guy or is it fear of injury if she refuses?

In the human world, it sounds like what goes on around some sports celebrities.

Leks

The Goulds tell us that, "Reproductively ready males gather into a concentrated 'chorus' for the sole purpose of providing a convenient place for females to come and select males to mate with. In general, lek territories are very small and clustered tightly together, and contain no resources for females. The males usually display continuously, which defends their patch and attracts potential mates .... The lek is a rare social system that turns up almost unpredictably in various species of flies, moths, bats, antelope, and birds."

In the human world, we see this in pick-up bars.

Social Hierarchies

When members of a group can recognize one another individually, it is likely that a pecking order will surface. Honeybees don't, but big horn sheep do, and in the latter case, dominance rituals are a regular feature of the culture. The Goulds report that dominance can be achieved by cleverness, through alliances, as well as by fighting. The individual at the top of the hierarchy will generally get to mate with most of the female herd. Only if there is more than one female ready at the same time do the second-ranking get a chance.

Sounds like politics to me.

Sublease Systems

Tigers do it and so do redwing blackbirds. In the sublease system, the guy defends a large area and a group of gals (independently) defend their own patch within the larger area. The guy has an investment in the kids, but he splits his time among more than one interest.

In the human world, some might call this animal behavior polygamy or adultery. Others might say these animals are married to their work. I can hear one of the females calling out, "You love the computer more than you love me!" I don't know, but there is something about this lifestyle that holds some appeal ....

Male Matrix
One of my favorite animal lifestyles is what the Goulds refer to as the "male matrix" organization, a subset of the resource-defense harem lifestyle. This behavior is found in animals ranging from dragonflies all the way to primates. It includes some African antelope such as the gazelle, impala, and wildebeest.

They report, "Males guard feeding territories, and females collect together into a herd for protection against predators. Because the males are not able to defend an area large enough to support the herd (either because the female herd is too large or the resources too diffuse), the females wander at will through the matrix, eating as they go. The resident male favored by the females at any one moment does his best to keep them on this property and mates with any that become reproductively receptive during their stay."

So, basically, the guys set up shop and mark their boundaries. Females have choice and stroll between boundaries (the guys never cross the lines), and wherever they find themselves when they are ready to mate is where they mate. Bachelor herds take the poorer or more dangerous areas. Defeated males also show up there, old males retire there, and the young come there to practice fighting.

In the human world, I can relate to this one because up until the age of thirty-eight I was sure I didn't want children. My sisters had both called during the previous years saying, "We're having the garage sale. Are you sure we shouldn't save the kid stuff for you?" "Sell it," I said. "I am so totally and completely sure."

Then I hit thirty-eight and every month, for two days (as I was ovulating), I would cry, "I have to have a baby!" Then I'd be fine the next twenty-six days until the next round when I would cry, "But who will want to look at my photos?" At first, Jack said no way. He was already forty-nine and had a daughter who was twenty-five—been there, done that. I said, "Okay then, I'll have to ask someone else." I had two guys in mind. Because "I have to have a baby!" It was beyond me. Intellectually, I still didn't really want to make the compromises I knew I would have to make, the sacrifices I knew would lie in my future. But it was beyond me, and all the intellectualizing didn't change that fact that each month I was feeling *I had to have a baby!*

Jack makes great kids so I have no regrets that he is the dad. By the way, neither does Jack. Seeing how much he loves David and how much they enjoy each other is a sight to behold. And the truth is, it just happened to be his male matrix I found myself in when I was "reproductively receptive" at age thirty-eight. Okay, maybe the angels had something to do with it, too.

Family of Choice

*I don't believe an accident of birth makes people
sisters or brothers. It makes them siblings, gives them
mutuality of parentage. Sisterhood and brotherhood
is a condition people have to work at.*

~ Maya Angelou, poet, memoirist,
actress and Civil Rights activist

HERE IN COLORADO, ONLY FORTY-FIVE PERCENT
of the population is made up of native Coloradoans. That
means that more than half the residents have left their
place of birth to make Colorado their home. Many of those have
also left their families of origin. I am one of those statistics. My
entire family resides back East. I regularly miss birthday celebra-
tions, holiday meals, and the informal hanging out that happens
for many families who live near each other. There is a void in my
life where family would be, but people need family and necessity
is the mother of invention. So here in Colorado, many of us have
created families of choice.

Some of the members of my family of choice are other families, like Dodi, her husband Daniel, and her two grown children,
Kevin and Andrew. While Dodi and I were friends ten years
ago, she was one of the first people to learn that I was pregnant
and that intimacy clinched the family of choice deal. At home,
we call Dodi and her family "beloveds," although out in the
world we refer to Dodi as David's godmother. Dodi is the first
local person I call when I have news, be it good or bad. She is
listed as first emergency contact on all our forms. Before David's
big sister, Nisa, got married and settled, Dodi was guardian for
David in the (God forbid) event that something were to happen
to me and Jack.

Dodi has a daycare center and once a week David works

there. In 2007, the Rockies made it to the playoffs and Daniel got sought-after tickets and took David to a game. We always celebrate birthdays and Hanukah together and, if we're in town, all the other holidays. I wouldn't hesitate to call on them if I needed something and I would expect the same from them.

Other members of my family of choice are sisters of choice. There are so many women whom I consider sisters of choice that I cannot even begin to list them. As it turns out, there may be a very old biological basis for this tendency of mine.

In 2000, Shelley E. Taylor, who runs a lab at UCLA, published an academic paper entitled "Biobehavioral Responses to Stress in Females: Tend-and-Befriend, Not Fight-or-Flight." Evidently, the fight-or-flight response is mostly a guy thing and until recently, most of the studies on it were made up mostly of men. Now that there are more women being counted, we've found out that the female response to stress differs. When women are threatened, they are spurred on by the release of the female hormone oxytocin and its interaction with estrogen. The effect on the system is to take care of self and offspring and to gather together with other women to do so. Shelley reports, "Across the entire life cycle, females are more likely to mobilize social support, especially from other females, in times of stress. They seek it out more, they receive more support, and they are more satisfied with the support they receive." As Robin Morgan said, "Sisterhood is powerful."

Although a handful of my sisters of choice are local, most do not live where I live. I still feel the void and am always on the prowl for more sisters. And now that Jack has moved out of state, an uncle of choice or two wouldn't hurt.

You might think that members of families of choice have fewer struggles or less devotion than families of origin, but that is not necessarily true. Take my friendship with Jessica as an example.

It was a Thursday in February, in the year 2000. I had just had a two-hour meeting in a friend's hot tub, and as I got out, I was thinking that it felt like I had been in there too long—I was literally too relaxed. I went to pick up David from preschool and as he and I left the building, he realized he forgot his baseball batting gloves.

We went back in, me on the right and David on the left.

As we entered, I headed left to where the teachers were, thinking I'd ask them if they had seen the gloves. David went to the right, evidently with his own unexpressed idea of where the gloves were. I stopped short to avoid colliding with him. As I did so, I caught the rubber toe of my new felt clog and fell over. I looked down and discovered that my left foot was hanging in a very peculiar fashion. The pain was inexpressible.

The next twenty-four hours were like a dream. Cindy, one of the directors at Plymouth, was going to call Jack, but he was out of town—in New York—until Sunday. Penny, the mom of triplets in David's class, took one look at me and said, "I'll take David home with me." Kathy, the other director, quickly got her coat and keys and said, "I'll take you to the ER."

In the emergency room, I moaned and groaned with delirious pain like I had *never* experienced. Childbirth paled in comparison. After what felt like hours of waiting for X-ray results, the incompetent ER doc said it was sprained and was going to send me home with an ace bandage. I said to him, "Are you crazy? My foot is hanging!" He suggested that maybe I might want go to the Orthopedic Center of the Rockies. I did. Kathy hung in there with me.

It was a different scene at the Orthopedic Center. Within a few minutes of my arrival, I had more X-rays taken. This time the diagnosis was that I had broken three bones in my foot—no, not broken, but shattered. The doctor said it looked as if a 400-pound anvil had fallen from above. Perhaps my bones and muscles had indeed got "too relaxed" in the hot tub and lost their sense of purpose.

Within a few minutes of the X-rays being read, I was given a general anesthesia and wheeled into surgery. They put two pins in my foot and placed me in a cast, which I would stay in—in one form or another—for the next eleven weeks. They insisted that I stay overnight at the Center, just to be sure everything was okay after the surgery.

At some point right after the surgery (I think it was after the surgery), Dodi showed up with David and said she'd keep him overnight. The next day, still quite drugged and recovering from the anesthesia and mild shock, Dodi came with David and told me that Jessica had offered to have me and David stay with her and her family for the weekend.

Now, out of context, this just seems like something one good friend would do for another. But there was a strong mitigating context: My friendship with Jessica, while once incredibly close and strong (when I'd call on the phone, her daughter used to shout, "Mom, it's your best friend!") was, at that time, strained. More accurately, I would say it was estranged. It had been three years since there had been any real communication between us.

But Jessica, a deep soul sister, pushed that right out of the way. "Who cares about that?" I imagine she said to herself. To me she said, "I can't imagine you spending the weekend—just you and David—in your house. Come to our house. We'll feed you. My kids will play with David. You can sleep or whatever."

And that's just what happened. I don't know how I would have managed at home. We got to Jessica's house Friday afternoon. I spent nights in the guest room while David had a sleepover in Jessica's son's room. During the days, I lay on the couch—drugged and quiet. I don't remember much although I do remember that I didn't even brush my hair. I didn't know where my son was or what he was doing but I wasn't worried. He was with family.

How was it that Jessica could respond with such compassion and empathy when we were so out of each other's lives? What is it that binds our souls and holds our hearts together?

To this day, I am overwhelmed with gratitude—gratitude for Jessica's generosity of spirit and for her openness of heart. I am grateful most of all for how she went above and beyond and, in the process, not only restored our friendship but also solidified us as family of choice.

My "Family" in Costa Rica

*To cement a new friendship, especially between foreigners or
persons of a different social world, a spark with which both
were secretly charged must fly from person to person,
and cut across the accidents of place and time.*

~ Cornelia Otis Skinner, author and actress

WHEN DAVID WAS FIVE, I TOOK HIM TO Costa Rica for three months. His English language acquisition was off the charts and I figured that while the going was good, I'd get another language in that rapidly developing brain of his. I also desperately needed an adventure.

In the letters I wrote to friends and family during that time, I unknowingly touched a deep place in the souls of the people on my personal e-mail list. It was something primordial, a yearning for simpler times, for more connectedness between generations. The response from my friends and family was "Please keep writing," and "I can smell the smells." "More, more!" My friend Shoshana, whom I hadn't seen for a few years, added, "With your letters, I feel intimately connected to you!"

That correspondence was a wonderful way to stay connected to people, and in some cases, to develop even new bonds of intimacy. When I break it down, it was really just storytelling. Maybe that's the primordial piece. For so many generations, grandparents and other elders in the community provided a context for storytelling, a grounding in what came before. With the destruction of the intergenerational experience for most North Americans, our roots have atrophied. We are missing the stories that give us a sense of roots and with those roots we could grow with confidence into who we were to become.

I share with you my first letter from Costa Rica:

Dear Friends,

After some (major) adjustments, we have finally landed in quasi-paradise. We are living with a family that is near perfect for us—a Grandmother (Chavella), Mother (Rosa), and her 16-year-old wonderful son, Jeremy. Rosa is one of 8 brothers/sisters, most of whom live in the same block. There are 18 grandchildren between the ages of 3 and 25 and a half dozen of the younger ones are in and out of the houses throughout the day. David has gotten comfortable enough to wander with the gang. Our bags of Legos have been a big hit and a daily happening. Right now, David is outside with three of the grandkids, chasing a chicken.

It turns out that my Spanish is better than I thought. Most people understand much of what I am trying to say and it is not so frequent that I have to ask people to speak more slowly. However, yesterday in class, I reviewed the subjunctive tenses (it's been 30 years since I last looked at those!) and it put it over the top for me. Remember the subjunctive? Here are like 13 categories of when to use it and it turns out it is about ninety percent of my conversations. All that thinking about how to say it …. I stop talking altogether. So, after four days of private classes, I am taking a break to allow for some integration.

David has had a slow start with the Spanish. I think it is because in English he has always liked so much to tell the *whole* story—not just "the cup," but rather "the plastic blue cup that is on top of the television, next to the book that Daddy bought yesterday at Barnes and Noble, when we were on our way to …." We have been talking about "shortcuts" and how it is okay to use two or three words and lots of hand motions. We've also talked about David's concern that by learning Spanish, he will forget English.

As you can imagine, we are having *"muchas experiencias"*—David fished and caught a trout, which we ate for lunch, and we have seen plants with leaves more than three feet wide. It has been a bit hard getting used to all the fried food and the plumbing conditions (throw *all* paper in the wastebasket next to the toilet, no paper in the toilet). The past few days I have helped prepare hundreds of empanadas from scratch, grinding *maize cascado* (corn without its skin) to make empanadas for *Semana Santa* (Holy Week).

The town is surrounded by green hills of coffee plants and when the sun sets, you can feel the tranquility blanketing the whole town. As the Costa Ricans say, *"Pura Vida."*

We are thinking of you and hope you and your circles are well. We send you blessings and best wishes for a spring blossoming with the renewal of life and spirit.

Love and Hugs,
Sarah and David

During the course of those three months, and the three visits since then, David and I became intimately connected with our host family. Little by little, we learned about their lives, and little by little, we shared about ours. Each encounter, another sister or brother would open up and share their thoughts and feelings about the changes happening in their family and in the country. With each conversation we would reveal deeper parts of ourselves. Maybe it was the vulnerability of speaking only in Spanish, or the leisure of having no appointments, along with a genuine, mutual feeling of *simpático**, but increasingly the line between "host family" and "family" blurred.

By our second visit, it all felt very natural. Rosa and I would often discuss strategies for single moms and, out of curiosity,

---

* Loosely translated as "likableness."

ask each other questions about each other's cultures. She and I had grown a deep sense of respect, admiration and empathy for each other, and genuinely enjoyed each other's company. Gabi, the sister-in-law next door—knowing that sunset is my favorite color—would send her son, Fabrisio, to get me when there was a particularly beautiful one. Andrés, the second eldest grandson and I had intimate conversations about the tension between following ones passion and the need to earn a living.

By our third visit, our "host" Rosa didn't want to take any money from me for our room and board and Elena and I were having ongoing conversations about childhood development (our boys are around the same age). Flori felt compelled to take us to the site of the deadly mudslide that had claimed a dozen lives just a few months before. She wanted us to know what this town had gone through. She walked with us along the path of the slide as she shared the story, processed the trauma and mourned the death of her village-mates.

But it was with Chavella, the grandmother of the clan, that my intimate connection with this family was sealed. Although actually younger than my mother, Chavella felt like a grandmother to me. Her stories filled in me a void—an emptiness left by not having had the passing on of stories from grandparents of my own. And for Chavella, it was a different kind of intimacy she had with me than that she had with her children or grandchildren. There was something very special about looking back, reflecting on the events of the past twenty-five years, and having an engaged, compassionate, and patient listener. But it didn't start out that way...

At first, it was very difficult for me to connect with Chavella. Not for a lack of want, but rather due to the language barrier. There is a rhythm and cadence in Chavella's speech that is beautiful—the words sound like poetry and flow together like streams of fresh sparkling water. Her "r"s have a "rsch" sound so when David calls to her and others would answer "*Si, mi amor*" (yes, my love), Chavella answers, "*Si, mi amorsch.*" Often the end of a word is lost as it merges with the next and it is only after I had moments to internally repeat the sentence that it made sense. By that time, the conversation would likely have moved onto other things—the moment to connect, lost. So although we smiled at each other all the time, it was simply very difficult for me to understand her.

It was a happy day when I got into the groove with Chavella's cadence and had my first conversation with her. It felt that suddenly I could understand everything she was saying, and from then on, Chavella and I talked all the time. Over the months and years, as her story unfolded, through her telling and through stories told to me by her children, I came to realize what an incredibly strong woman she is. We trusted each other, and with that trust and the affluence of time, we revealed ourselves to each other.

I learned that Chavella was the eldest daughter of thirteen brother and sisters. When she finished the third grade, it was the end of her formal education. At nine years old, she joined her mother, a seamstress, helping her sew clothes for everyone in town. The town was smaller then. There was no electricity or indoor plumbing in the town, and everyone was poor. It was just before the coffee boom—up until then coffee was grown, picked and roasted for personal use, from bushes in one's own backyard. There was a spring of warm water in the backyard where she and her brothers and sisters would go to wash themselves. The children had no shoes. They had four or five beds with three children arranged in each. At some point, someone in town bought a machine for making shoes and Chavella's father bought her first pair. Given their precious nature they were reserved for Sundays only.

She married at eighteen. I heard stories about each of the births of her eight children and then about how, thirty-two years later, her husband left her for a woman half his age. Only he didn't just leave her; he abandoned his *whole* family. This was a big scandal in the town. He had been a man of wealth, dignity, and prestige, very straight ahead and correct in his dealings. In the twenty-plus years since he left, he has had virtually no contact with any member of his family. He did not attend the weddings of his two youngest daughters and has never met most of his 20 grandchildren.

Elena, the youngest daughter, cried when she told me about

how her father didn't come to her wedding. She pulled out the photo albums and showed me the invitation and the pictures and described her personal wound of the abandonment. The youngest son, Luis, told me how he felt betrayed and suspected something magical like witchcraft lies behind his father's deserting. He knew of many cases of trouble between spouses leading to separation and divorce—and even estrangement—with one or two children who have acted badly. But estrangement from *all* children and *all* grandchildren…?

Chavella's also spoke to me of her family of origin, her twelve sisters and brothers, and how most of them and their children had been working at the *balnearios* (thermal pools) that Chavella's father had built from that warm spring in the backyard. It had become quite a large and lucrative business with pools, a restaurant, and a playing field. Most worked there without formal salaries, expecting a share of the family business. But Chavella's mother, while on her deathbed, had signed the whole business over to one of her sons, and suddenly, almost violently, for a majority of Chavella's family, their source of support was uncertain, their inheritance was denied, and their family system was all but destroyed. The resentment and estrangement is apocrypha in this town.

Chavella revealed these stories not all at once, but bit by bit, over the years as we became family. You might expect that among her children you'd find signs of rancor, threads of the estrangement with each other. But somehow this never happened. I attribute this to Chavella's faith and positive, evolved outlook on life. Chavella says—and I believe her—that she holds no rancorous feelings toward her husband. She feels bad for, albeit somewhat removed from, the troubles among her siblings. Chavella proclaims that all these things are in the hands of God and that she is content with her lot. Her life is full with her wide array of gardening in the backyard, events with the seniors, and the general living with and caring for her children and grandchildren. She sighs and she smiles, and then she moves on.

Years ago, at the age of sixty-four, Chavella taught herself to swim. Now, she goes almost every day to swim in the thermal pools—in what was her childhood backyard—often taking a handful of grandchildren with her. They let her in for free.

At the end of the three months of our first visit, Chavella had purchased a stack of plastic Disney dessert plates for the younger grandchildren and was writing the name of each on the undersides. "This one is for Estéfano and this one is for Gastón," she said as she wrote. On the last one, she said, "And this one is for David." It was official. We were family.

Family of Circumstance

'Strangers,' the Blue Man said, 'are just family
you have yet to come to know.'

~ Mitch Albom, author,
in *The Five People You Meet in Heaven*

THE MORE I SPEAK WITH PEOPLE ABOUT THEIR intimacy constellations, the more stories I hear about what I call "family of circumstance"—people who come into our lives at unexpected moments or for unexpected reasons and who become, on some level that transcends DNA, family. My neighbor, Leeanne, has a child, Dane, who is deaf. Leeanne told me about a deaf young man, Henri, who serendipitously came into their lives just when Dane's hearing impairment was discovered. And then there's my friend who doesn't have a close relationship with her mother or father, but while she was dating in high school, she developed an intimate connection with her boyfriend's parents. Although they are no longer dating—truth be told, they aren't speaking to each other—her ex-boyfriend's parents are still in relationship with her and call her "the other daughter."

I have a whole set of people who are in my life solely related to the circumstance that I was married to Jack. Sometimes those "ex" and "step" relationships can be tricky. In our case, we are like the poster children for blended families. In my life, it's people like Nisa, my ex-step daughter, and her mother, Susan, who begin to comprise my family of circumstance. Susan and Jack split when Nisa was one and a half. Nisa was eighteen when her Dad and I got engaged. We were living in Philadelphia and she was living with her mother in Canada, where she had grown up. My relationship with Nisa's mother developed before the one with Nisa.

When Jack and I got married, Nisa was about to go off to college. I had talked with Jack about how we should offer to pay for half the college expenses and had asked him if he had yet had that conversation with Susan. No, he hadn't, he admitted. He made the call and left a message. When Susan called back, unknowingly (before caller ID), I picked up. After a few pleasantries, Susan said, "Sarah, I hope you don't mind if I talk with you about this. I've never been terribly comfortable talking with Jack about money, and I'm sure you put him up to it anyway." Not that Jack isn't generous. We both know he is. It's just we also both know that he wouldn't have thought of it, in advance, of his own accord. Instantly, Susan and I became good friends. Just a few years later, we became family. While she is still friendly with my/her ex, she told me years ago to make no mistake that she loves me. She knows the feeling is mutual.

Nisa is now thirty-five, lives in Canada, is married, and has two young children of her own. They are my son's niece and nephew. They call me Nana. Nisa is the identified guardian for her "little brother" should anything, God forbid, happen to me and her dad. To this day, my relationship with Nisa and her family is profoundly important to me. We decided years ago that it didn't matter if I stayed married to her dad or not; we would still be in each other's lives. She credits me with bringing her dad back into her life, and she and I speak on the phone at least once a month, sometimes for a really long time. We share stories about her little brother and the grandkids, and I hear all about how she is navigating her life with two little ones. Lucky for us, we also have lots of common interests, and we always have more to talk about than we have time for. Once or twice a year, I go with David to Canada to visit. While there, we stay with Nisa and her family. In a prime example of the "family of circumstance" carousel, her husband Matthew is a great big brother to David.

We were all together for the Passover Seder a few years ago, including Jack, Susan's new wonderful man friend, a tribe of half-siblings and step-siblings, and Nisa's in-laws, who are doing an admirable job of taking it all in. Jack and I are making plans to overlap in Canada for our grandson's birthday, and we are all hoping that his new girlfriend (a terrific woman—he just keeps finding terrific women) will join us.

And then there's the donor family. Remember that seventeen years ago, Jack was a sperm donor for our friend, Julie, in Philadelphia. She now has five children—three biological (including two from Jack) and two adopted from Guatemala. I don't know how she does it, but she manages to spend quality "special" private time with each child every week. The eldest just went off to Brown University as the youngest went into first grade. Being Jack's offspring, two of her kids are half siblings of my son. The elder of the adopted kids is a boy David's age. Julie is co-parenting the younger children with a man in her community—but not living with him—who very much wanted a family of his own but for whom that didn't happen in a biological way. They all live near my parents, so we see them at least two or three times a year. Julie is the next in line, after Nisa, to care for David if, God forbid, something happened. We call them all God family.

Each of these stories could have easily had a different ending. We live far enough away from all these folks that it could have been that our paths would never cross. But as Susan said, "The most important thing that makes us friends and family ... we have become an extended family by opening our hearts to each other. And we all gain from that intimacy."

As we're fond of showing, there are lots of ways to make a family.

Trauma

Accept the things to which fate binds you,
and love the people with whom fate brings you together,
but do so with all your heart.

~ Marcus Aelius Aurelius, Roman emperor, philosopher

JACK IS A CHILD OF HOLOCAUST SURVIVORS. HE was born in 1946, in Italy, in a camp for displaced persons at the end of World War II.

His parents' stories are very dramatic. His mother, Mathilde, had hidden in an attic with a small group of people for eighteen months, with only brief forays out into the fresh air. During one of those infrequent jaunts, she found her parents dead in the street and buried them herself. She was twenty-one.

Oh My God.

Jack's father, Junik, survived two death camps. At one, he had been lined up against the wall, with the others, in front of the mass grave they had dug. The soldiers fired their guns and, by some twist of fate, they missed Junik. He didn't let on, closed his eyes and fell into the grave with the dead bodies. A short time later, he climbed out and hopped the fence. They came after him with dogs. He hid under water for hours, breathing through a reed. The water was full of leeches and he spent the next six months in a barn of some sympathetic Polish farmers in the countryside, recovering from blood poisoning.

Oh My God.

Later that year, Junik and Mathilde reunited in their home-town in Poland. They had been childhood sweethearts and were ecstatic to find each other alive. During their brief reunion in Poland, a Russian solider visited the town to conscript all able men into the Czar's army. Junik and Mathilde got him drunk, knocked him unconscious, and fled.

Oh My God.

With Junik's facility with languages and his engaging demeanor, he and Mathilde crossed border after border until they came to the camp set up for displaced persons in Santa Maria de Lioca, in the heel of Italy. Mathidle was pregnant and the young couple applied for visas to emigrate to Palestine (Israel had not yet been declared a State). At that time, immigration was limited, but there was one category that had priority: pregnant women.

Soon, the newlyweds had tickets and visas, and everything was in order. A few days before their planned departure, the "administrator" of the camp visited with Junik and Mathilde, telling them that he needed their tickets and visas in order to process their departure. Later that day, he sold them to someone else.

Oh My God.

A few months later, Jack was born and spent the first three years of his life in the DP camp.

I do not begin to claim to really know what it is like to grow up with this kind of traumatic family history. Although my mother is a child of survivors of the pogroms in Russia, her stories are nothing like this one.

However, it is in my nature to analyze everything, and the behavior of children of survivors is no exception. And being married to a child of survivors for fifteen years and organizing conferences in the Jewish community, I have become very conscious and sensitive to the impact of the Holocaust on children of survivors. I can spot them a mile away.

In my analysis, there are two characteristics I've found to be true for all survivors and children of survivors I've met. The first characteristic is that whatever their *schtick* is, they have it more. If they like to cook or want to feed you, there will be three choices of soups, four entrees, a salad large enough to feed an army, and seven pies for dessert. If they are savers, they will have twelve boxes of scrap paper that they have been *schlepping* around for twenty-five years, along with the bags of rubber bands and twist ties because "you never know when you'll need them." When they were refugees looking for a new place to live, they didn't just settle anywhere; they established a country (Israel) with a government and social services, and they declared it home for all Jewish refugees.

The second impressive characteristic is the level of instant intimacy. It is the Intimacy of Shared Trauma. It is similar to the intimacy that happens for soldiers who have experienced war and for members of any 12-step program of recovery. It is immediate and it is strong. Instant family. "War stories" are shared and compared, not with a sense of competition—my hurt is bigger than yours— but rather with a deep understanding and empathy of shared experience that cannot be adequately expressed in words and cannot be understood by others who have not shared the experience.

Genuine Generosity

In memory of Mathilde Schechtman *z"l* *

I expect to pass through this world but once. Any good
therefore that I can do, or any kindness that I can show
to any fellow creature, let me do it now. Let me not
defer or neglect it, for I shall not pass this way again.

~ William Penn, early champion of democracy
and religious freedom in America

A FEW YEARS AGO, I TOLD JACK THAT I THOUGHT
we should tell his mom about the kids that were born
with Jack as the donor. We were a little concerned about
her response because she'd been pretty unpredictable until then.
However, it just seemed right that someone who had barely survived the Holocaust ought to know that there were two more of
her progeny in the world.

So one day, we were visiting her in her Brooklyn apartment, sitting on the sofa with the plastic slipcovers, and I said, "Mathilde,
do you know that your son did a very generous thing? He donated
his sperm to a woman who really wanted children who isn't married. She has two children who came from Jack's sperm." And then
we were quiet. Would she be upset? Would she turn to Jack and tell
him that it's craziness to do such a thing? Would she accuse him of
being irresponsible?

Without flinching, Mathilde replied, "Oh, really? His father
did something like that. When we were in the DP camp, there was
an old man with tuberculosis who really wanted to go to Israel, but
you know they didn't want to let him in because of the tuberculo-

---

* *z"l* is an abbreviation for the Hebrew *zihron livracha*—may her memory be for
a blessing.

sis. My husband gave the man his own chest x-rays."

Lesson learned?... Don't ever assume you know the outcome of a conversation until is has happened.

Alternatives to Marriage/ Alternatives to Divorce

*Sometimes I wonder if men and women really suit
each other. Perhaps they should live next door
and just visit now and then.*

~ Katherine Hepburn, actress

MARRIAGE IS ABOUT EXPECTATIONS, disappointment, commitment, and perseverance. It's about joy, friendship, sex, compromise, partnership, and family. It's about playfulness, trust and sharing and listening. It's about connection, vulnerability, integrity, and honesty. And, as is often true with time and money, we also tend to focus on what isn't working in a marriage rather than the abundance or potential relationship that is staring us in the face.

People sometimes equate loneliness with being alone. For me, the opposite is often true. I am rarely lonely when I am alone. Given that I can, in the blink of an eye, open myself to the intimacy of time, space, nature, and spirit, and to the thoughts of the intimate relationships that enrich my life, solitude just doesn't make me feel alone. In fact, some of the most memorable lonely moments I have felt have been when in a crowded room. Honestly, the loneliest memories of my life are from the period of time when I was married. Just as the definition of intimacy is being seen, heard, or understood, loneliness is the absence of that.

Having said that, I don't think of my relationship with Jack as a failed marriage. I look around me at the richness of relationships that are in my life because of my connection with Jack—his daughter, her mother, her children; the "donor" family; the richness of intimacies with the *Rosh Hodesh* group in Fort Collins. There are intimacies Jack and I still share. On the lighter side, we love the same foods and the same movies. We are also both committed to the Jewish concept of *Tikkun Olam* (repairing the world). Jack is a gifted singer/songwriter and when I first met him, I fell in love with his music. His melodies penetrate to the heart, and his lyrics reveal a simple brilliance. Through his music, I feel a deeper knowing of the human soul.

Jack is still, absolutely, an intimate part of my family. The difference is his position has shifted from immediate family to "family of circumstance." He is the father of my only child and he is a good guy who means well and tries hard. I am delighted to call him my friend.

What the shift means is that I am no longer committed to be a knowing witness on a daily basis. So too, I no longer expect him to knowingly witness my journey on a daily basis. However, after fifteen years of living together and being that daily knowing witness, I don't stop knowing him. I know when he's going to be late and I know when he's withholding information. I know how much he puts out to do a public event, how nourished he is by the applause, and how deeply exhausted he is afterwards. I also know that if I make an extra portion of dinner and give it to him that I will make his day.

Although I speak to him every few days, I have limits on the topics of conversation. I am careful around areas that put me in a vulnerable place, for example, the internal processing of my thoughts, and analysis of what is making me tick. I have also asked him not to share his self-processing with me. But I do share with him, freely, my thoughts and analysis of what makes our son tick. We regularly process together the experiences our son has and how they might be affecting his physical, emotional, intellectual, and spiritual growth.

The intimacies we do share are not the building blocks I needed in the foundation for a marriage partner. Stepping aside the question of whether I even want the long-term, monogamous, committed, share-my-daily-life intimacy of what most of us think of as marriage—if I were to want that, I would be looking for a different list of intimate connections. This is by no means any kind of generic list. It is my list, specific to my stories, my wounds, my gifts. It is based on what I am able to give and what I am able to receive. I'd like to think that the list won't change tomorrow, but I can't be sure about that.

In any event, just because a marriage ends doesn't mean the relationship on which it was built ceases to exist. The marital intimacy I shared with Jack, in many ways, endures long after the formal and legal dissolution of our wedded status. Indeed it continues to evolve as we both bring new people into our widening family of circumstance.

Intimate Challenges

The attitude we take into a social interaction will be catching. If we are confrontational, the other person is likely to be the same. If we are not really interested in connecting, they probably won't also. If we approach the interaction seeking deep connection and coming from our compassionate centre, they will also want the same thing.

~ CL Claridge, www.slowmovement.com,
Mooloolaba, Australia

Yearning for More

*How different our lives are when we really know what is
deeply important to us, and, keeping that picture in mind,
we manage ourselves each day to be and to know
what really matters most.*

~ Stephen Covey, author

JULIET AND I HAVE BEEN FRIENDS FOR THIRTY-nine years, ever since that day in fourth grade when we were ten years old (okay, she was nine, I was ten) when Juliet came to visit the school. She was transferring from private school to public school and Mrs. Lanard had asked me to show her around.

In those early years, we shared lots of experiences like climbing trees and playing kickball. We also witnessed developmental milestones like kissing boys and buying bras. Even though Juliet moved to New Orleans when we were fifteen (okay, she was fourteen, I was fifteen), we have remained dear, beloved friends. At some point, she moved back to Philly; then I left and came back again, only to depart again for Colorado sixteen years ago. We've shared lots of experiences in those thirty-nine years—from streaking in the early 1970s and Mardi Gras madness through marriage, children and thoughtful spiritual growth as we approach fifty. Throughout it all the one constant has been … junk food … oh, I mean the one constant has been a commitment to share and witness—with love and support and without judgment—the unfolding of our lives.

The physical distance part of staying connected was always more challenging for Juliet than for me. I can do daily connection across 1,500 miles. I do that with my parents now, checking in with them almost every day, but I understand that not everyone can. Juliet and I still track the big things. When I got pregnant, divorced, things like that, Juliet was on my short list of people whom I thought to tell along with my family of origin.

Yet, I have often yearned for more frequent contact. There are so few people with who I share so many intimate connections— shared values, shared experiences, shared interests, shared love of cheese doodles—I want to be more regularly connected. I've had to accept that my relationship with Juliet is not going to satisfy that slice of my intimacy pie—that place where I'm tracking the regular, daily, or weekly movements of someone's life.

It's disappointing and I used to feel that disappointment deeply. I would think of how we're not in touch more often and I would feel lonely. When I analyze my friendship with Juliet, she comes in strong in more "intimacy categories" than anyone else. When I think of my friendship with Juliet, my soul sings Hallelujah. Yet, the yearning for more lowers the volume.

Being a single woman, I notice that this void in Daily Tracking Intimacy comes up periodically. Sometimes, in the deeper moments of yearning, I think, "Oh, I need to be married," and while I'm not against the possibility, I realize that that would be a pretty drastic way to satisfy the need for a little daily tracking. What I do instead is look at the bright side—what I have with Juliet (and others). We have a kind of "slumber party" intimacy that is reminiscent of overnight camp days. I see her when I am in Philadelphia. Sometimes we spend twenty-four hours together, eating junk food, talking all night about everything, going skinny-dipping, and then eating more junk food. We've known each other so long, loved each other for so many years, that our conversations can be just about as intimate as it gets. Even though Juliet is not in my daily, weekly, or even monthly circles, I am deeply nourished by my connection with her.

Another example is my friend Naomi. Naomi and I have a unique friendship. Our mothers were both in therapy when we were growing up (they get the pioneer badge of courage for doing this in the early sixties), and so we both grew up in households where psychological language was the norm. When I met Naomi, she was pregnant with her second child and, as is often the case with mothers of young children, it was difficult for her to have any long phone conversations. In the four years that we have been friends, we have had deep, honest, intimate conversations for seven minutes at a time, once a week if we are lucky. No chit-chat for us—it's directly to one of us saying, "Here's how I'm struggling with my shadow right now" while the other acts as witness, challenger, and reflector. What a gift, and at the same time, it stimulates a yearning for more.

Sometimes it feels that nearly everyone I love is far away. I've traveled all over the world and made so many intimate connections—Miyuki in Japan, Caroline in Egypt and now in Toronto, Michal in Vancouver, Rosa's family in Costa Rica. I want my parents around the corner and my sisters around the block. I want my son to have cousins he knows intimately and plays with all the time. I want that part of time to go back to when neighborhoods were neighborhoods. In Costa Rica, we scored big time when we landed with that extended family. My whole family of origin lives in Philadelphia, but I live 1,500 miles away in Colorado.

I have a fantasy that if I were to win the lottery, I would have a great big party and invite all my families—everyone who is a bright star in my intimacy constellation—from all over the world to be together. Everyone would meet each other and form their own connections. The web around us would just keep getting wider and stronger, forming into one big cosmic embrace.

Intimacy Denied

We're a crowd animal, a highly gregarious,
communicative species, but the culture
and the age and all the fear that fills our days
have put almost everyone into little boxes,
each of us all alone.

~ Anne Lamott, author of *Bird by Bird*

WITH ALL THIS OPTIMISTIC TALK ABOUT intimacy, I know that there are some of you cynical pessimists who say, "Hey, what about all the crappy interpersonal experiences? What about all those moments when it just ain't happening?"

To be sure, there are plenty of experiences that do not lend themselves to intimacy. Some are just neutral, while other experiences are downright anti-intimacy—moments when you are definitely NOT seen or heard or known or understood.

One of the most non-intimate experiences I can remember was a real-estate transaction. Jack and I were selling our two houses in Boulder (part of our "Alternative to Divorce" experiment of staying married while living in separate houses) and buying one house in Denver.

We priced the houses just right and pretty soon we had offers on both. Each buyer had an agent, so now, in addition to our Boulder agent and our Denver agent, we had these indirect relationships with the buyers' agents for the two different people buying our houses. As you can well imagine, our agents didn't really want us talking to their agents, thereby setting the stage for some major non-intimacy.

Then we had the even more indirect—no, more than indirect… more like disconnected relationships with the actual buyers. If one of the buyers had a question, he would ask his agent who would ask our agent who would, in turn, ask us. The answer, of course, would go back along that same route. Multiply that circuital disarray by two and you get a good idea of what we were enduring.

Simultaneously, we went through the same disconnection with the place we were buying in Denver. Buying agent + selling agent + seller somewhere in the hinterlands = intimacy denied.

At one point, I did manage to break through with one of those relationships. I met the man who was buying my house. He had young kids and wanted to know about the neighborhood. He came over with his offspring, and we chatted while the kids played in David's playroom. It felt good. Our agents were none too happy about it, but for me, it made all the difference in the world.

No offense to any individual real estate broker—each one that I've met has been nice enough to deal with—but the whole business is one of the few processes that seems to be set-up for low satisfaction from the human connection point of view.

Another way intimate connections are disrupted is through conflict avoidance. If you do something that is hurtful to me and I don't talk with you about it, I put a stop to our ability to have an intimate connection. I *do* avoid that uncomfortable moment of confrontation, but at a very high cost. Similarly, if I have done something that is hurtful to you, you confront me about it, and I respond defensively, I also put a stop to the flow of intimate connection.

I experienced this phenomenon first hand a few months after we moved to Denver for Jack's new job, which didn't work out. Well, it didn't just not work out. The whole organization fell apart. Being that I was a little invested in its success—we had uprooted our family—and given my set of entrepreneurial and management consultant skills, I offered to help. There were two women, let's call them Janie and Kathy, who worked with Jack and who, after my offer and without my knowledge, conspired to not talk to me. Did they feel threatened? Were they power hungry or simply controlling? Even after asking what was up, I never did really understand it. Honestly, what it felt like was that I was in seventh grade dealing with two mean girls—deeply stuck in adolescence—who wanted to exclude me.

Norwood Public Library
1110 Lucerne Street
Norwood, CO 81423

In the very end, it was like theater of the absurd. Picture this: Jack has been hospitalized with heart palpitations and dizziness the day he is supposed to decide about renewing his contract. Coincidently, it is David's birthday. I am on the phone with doctors and schoolteachers and childcare. Jack is getting more agitated, concerned about the meeting he's supposed to have with his board of directors the next day. I try to talk with these women to find out what is the best way to proceed and they refuse to talk to me. In the end, I call another board member—and I hear from him that these adolescent women have tried to get him not to talk with me either. Oh My God. Thankfully, he is a *mentsch* and a grown-up. He ignores them and helps me through that week.

A year later, during that wonderful time in the Jewish calendar when you do that "Please forgive me; I forgive you" stuff, I tried again to clear the blockage. Inspired by a note I had received from a friend during that same time, that read, "If I have done anything that has interrupted the connection between us, please let me know so we can clear it up," I sent a note to Janie. I let her know that the experience had been really hurtful for me and that I was sorry for my part. She responded with three terse, defensive sentences, ending any possibility of connection.

Sometimes, try as you might, it's just gonna feel yucky.

Intimacy Achieved

*It is easy to fly into a passion—anybody can do that—
but to be angry with the right person and at the right time
and with the right object and in the right way—
that is not easy, and it is not everyone who can do it.*

~ Aristotle, philosopher

WHILE SOMETIMES ATTEMPTED INTIMACY IS just gonna feel yucky, other times, there is breakthrough. Before I met Jack, Nancy (not her real name) had come into his life to help him heal his recently divorced, wounded soul. Nancy was currently out of an in-and-out relationship and was seeking her own kind of healing. Nancy *wanted* Jack. I knew it intuitively from how she watched him and winked at him, but at the time, Jack would not admit it.

I imagined that she felt threatened by me as she would regularly bring up experiences they had shared, all of which highlighted how much better and longer she knew him—what a big part of his picture she was—which naturally made me a small part of the picture. Jack flat out denied that their relationship had ever been anything but friends, and when I confronted Nancy, telling her that I was uncomfortable with how she seemed to want to pull Jack away from me, she tersely replied that that was between me and Jack and that I should talk to him about it. Around that same time, we moved and by consequence her pulling became less of an issue.

Flash forward a couple of years. In a very relaxed and intimate moment, Jack finally reveals that, yes, Nancy had wanted him. She had chased him around tables and come on pretty strong, again and again.

I was furious. I *knew* it. I was livid that he had lied about and denied it. I had been deceived and felt like a fool. I ranted and raved for days. Finally, my anger subsided. He hadn't cheated on me, I eventually realized. It had all transpired before he even knew me. I heard him and how at the time he had felt so wounded and confused about everything that he hadn't wanted to admit all the conflicting feelings. With his tail between his legs, he came clean. Forgiveness was just one of many lessons I learned while married.

Nancy, however, was a different story. She and Jack had been friends for many years and she was still in his life, although being a few states away, it was now just a phone relationship. Never-the-less, every time I heard her voice, or even her name, I felt sick. I felt especially disgusted by this deception revealed because Nancy put on the appearance of being a strong proponent of personal growth and integrity. I owed it to the world to make this confrontation.

I decided to write her a letter.

In the letter, I simply told her that Jack had confirmed what I knew then and what she and Jack had both denied. I went on to describe how although she put out that her relationship with Jack was all about his healing, her lack of support of my relationship with Jack—the private storytelling and exclusion—was really *not* supportive of him. Moreover, it was really not supportive of me. I pointed out how the deceit had continued to that day, where there was no sisterly flow of energy between us.

Her response to me was a combination of fake warmth and defensiveness. "No, really," she said, "I was supportive of you. I always told him that I thought it was good for him to be with you."

I persisted. "No, Nancy, that was not supportive of me. If you had been supportive of *me*, you would have made an effort to have a relationship with *me*. Each time you excluded me to make yourself closer to him, you made the gulf between us a little wider."

Back and forth we went, with her saying, "Oh, but no," and my saying, "I don't think so" until she finally got it. Like a light bulb going on, she finally saw it. Truthfulness and personal insight flowed as she expressed how her actions had been guided by her own unfulfilled need to be cherished. It wasn't sisterly, it wasn't in alignment with integrity, and I was right to be angry. She thoroughly copped to the whole picture and thanked me for hanging in.

The next time I saw Nancy, I was genuinely happy to see her. We made sure we had some time just for the two of us and took a walk. We didn't talk about the past—we didn't need to. In the end, with intimacy achieved, we had lots of the present to catch up on.

Organized Religious Intimacy

Ritual is necessary for us to know anything.

~ Ken Kesey, author

PEOPLE OFTEN CONFUSE RELIGION AND spirituality. Spirituality, for me, is about the interconnectedness of everything, a sense of being a part of the cosmic web of energy. Religion, on the other hand, is a set of practices that is supposed to—is, in fact, designed to—bring you onto the path of spirituality. Organized religion is our human attempt to guide large groups of people on that path together.

For this reason, organized religion is often a vortex for intimate moments, and a place where long-term intimate relationships are formed. Like the *Rosh Hodesh* group in Fort Collins, the religious rituals and practice create a sense of shared experience year after year.

But it doesn't always work that way for everyone.

To say that my relationship with Jewish practice is ambivalent is an understatement. I was married to a rabbi for fifteen years but almost never went to services. I love how the holidays follow the moon and I build a *sukkah* (harvest hut) in my backyard for that autumn holiday every year. I can't relate to the theology in the prayerbook at all, yet I know the traditions around death and dying are profound. So is the whole notion of the Sabbath. I'm sick of dealing with the Post Traumatic Stress Disorder of the Jewish people* yet my deepest friendships are with Jewish women.

Oy.

My relationship with the holiday of Passover (*Pesach*, in Hebrew—the "ch" is like something's stuck in your throat) is no

---

* After surviving 700 years of internalized and externalized oppression, it is not surprising that the Jewish people, as tribe, suffer the effects of trauma.

exception to the ambivalent thing. *Pesach* is supposed to be the ultimate in shared experience on many levels. Measuring participation, statistics show that ninety-five percent of people who identify as Jewish attend a *seder* (the Passover meal). That is a higher than at any other moment in the Jewish year. And considering that fifty percent of people who identify as Jewish aren't affiliated with any synagogue and generally don't really feel connected, that is a pretty impressive percentage of participation.

On the level of shared spiritual experience, on *Pesach* we are instructed that we should imagine that we, ourselves, were slaves in Egypt during the time of Moses, that we left Egypt and crossed the Red Sea, that we were there at Sinai and received the Ten Commandments, and that we wandered in the desert for forty years. During the *seder*, we re-enact the story from the ten plagues and tell the story of the exodus from Egypt. At this epitome of tribal empathy, we are supposed to feel that experience.

Here's the problem. The preparation that leads up to that moment in the *seder* does not support the goal. It is one of the few Jewish holidays that doesn't feel organic to its origins. The scientists would say it lacks "ecological validity." Take for example, *Shabbos* (the Sabbath). God rested on the seventh day so, okay, we rest on the seventh day. And *Sukkot*—we are remembering that our ancestors slept in huts at the harvest moon, so at the harvest moon, we build a *sukkah* in our backyard and for seven days we eat/sleep in it. That's ecological validity.

Now, consider Passover. On Passover, we remember the exodus from Egypt—how we were slaves in Egypt, and how we had to leave our homes—very fast and with only what we could carry on our backs, so fast they say the bread did not have time to rise (that's the matzah part). We ran especially fast because our sons were "passed over" and not affected by that awful tenth plague and we were afraid that Pharaoh would change his mind (which he did).

And how do we celebrate? By thoroughly, obsessively, and compulsively cleaning our kitchens to remove every last crumb of old stuff we can find, and by thoroughly, obsessively, and compulsively sealing our everyday dishes and cabinets and pantries to make sure any reminder of the crumbs is hidden away, and by thoroughly, obsessively, and compulsively schlepping out our Passover dishes and cooking accessories as if we don't have enough clutter already in our homes. And then, when we are thoroughly physically and psychically exhausted from all this, we cook a dinner for twenty guests, including at least a few people we don't know—and organize a *seder*—a meal with fourteen parts to it. Then the next night—second *seder*—we do it again. Like I said, totally lacking ecological validity.

I have a better idea.

How about, at 4:15 P.M. as the first night of Passover approaches, we ring a bell. Then we have thirty minutes to gather what we need for the next eight days. We cannot take more with us than we can carry ourselves. We have only thirty minutes and then we have to jump into our cars and drive an hour to the Y-Camp at Rocky Mountain National Park, where we gather with the rest of the tribe. We spend seven or eight days there together, and like the Israelites, we spend our time *kvetching* about what we left behind and expressing fear about what lies ahead. We have a potluck picnic with what we all brought. Whaddya think?

I've been trying to get folks to do this with me for years, but so far, I've gotten no takers. One year I decided to create my own slavery/exodus/liberation. On the first day of Passover, I invited my handyman, Gary, to start a refinishing-the-living-floor/replacing-the-kitchen-floor project. That meant I had to pack up everything in the living room and kitchen really fast so he could move all the furniture and start sanding. Then I was displaced from my kitchen for days and a fine dust from the sanding (reminiscent of the sand in the desert) lay all over everything in my house. He finished up just as the holiday came to a close. How liberating it was when the project was done. Now that's what I call ecological validity.

Objectification

Be who you are and say what you feel,
because those who matter don't mind,
and those who mind don't matter.

~ Dr. Seuss (Theodor Seuss Geisel), author

JACK AND I GOT MARRIED AUGUST 26, 1990, AND four days later, we moved to Wildwood, New Jersey. There, Jack became the rabbi of an established Jewish community serving the beach towns of Wildwood and Cape May.

The community was kind of "Reconservafusadox" in its practice. Most of the congregants earned their living from the tourist industry and therefore, as a rule, worked on the Sabbath. Many of them were survivors and children of survivors of the Holocaust. Thus, they had their own brand of craziness around Jewish identity. Some of them sort of kept kosher.

The community in New Jersey had previously been served, for twenty years, by a rigid, orthodox rabbi. It provided a parsonage—a house that was reserved for its members' clergy and family. The previous rabbi had kept strictly kosher and when invited to congregants' homes for dinner, the food needed to be prepared in his home in advance. This community knew they needed a change from the retiring rigid, orthodox guy, but they didn't really know what they wanted. Frankly, they were very sheltered Jewishly and they didn't really know what was available. Most of the people were very kind, but it was a hard year. You see, on his way out, the previous rabbi told his circle of ten loyal, every-Saturday-morning-synagogue-going men, "Don't trust this new guy." Thanks, rabbi.

During the less-than-a-year we spent there, Jack became the congregants' "crunch" rabbi—the guy who helps make the change happen but gets crushed in the process. Many churches, understanding this dynamic, have a designated job description for a temporary clergy person who is engaged to help in exactly this transition. We were green, however, and had no idea what was in store for us.

The relationships in a rabbi's life are complex. The transference that goes on between a rabbi and his flock is intense. To the congregants, their spiritual leader symbolizes God, and subconsciously, they want him to be like God—all knowing, all seeing, nearing perfection. If they are having problems—be they spiritual, marital, or financial—the rabbi should have the right answer. He should be more religious than they are and always doing good in the world. If he gets ill, everyone gets concerned. When he has something to celebrate, everyone wants to celebrate, too. Sometimes he is beloved and sometimes ... well, you know the joke about the rabbi who was in the hospital after a heart attack? The President of the Board came to visit and said, "Rabbi, the board would like to wish you a complete and speedy recovery. They voted on it, six to four."

As complex as the relationships are for the rabbi, at least they are somewhat direct. Or as I used to say to Jack, at least he gets paid to navigate through them. As for me, up until the age of thirty-three, I had been a powerful, independent, and accomplished single woman. Overnight, I became "The Rabbi's Wife" in a small town. I was totally unprepared.

There is actually a Hebrew word for the rabbi's wife: *rebbetzin.* Susan J. Landau-Chark, writing on perceptions of the role of *rebbetzin,* notes that one popular perception is that "Women married to rabbis should display 'devotion and counsel,' were 'faithful helpmates,' and 'blessed the [lives of their husbands] with children, courage, and confidence.'" And they should spend a lot of time in the kitchen.

In reality, people are confused about how they feel about the *rebbetzin.* When people asked me what it was like to be married to a rabbi, I would tell them to imagine that their spouse was a therapist and that all of their friends were made up of his patients. They'd either want to get on your good side to be closer to him

(God—that transference thing), speed right past you in their haste to get directly to him (God—that transference thing), or avoid you because they were one of the four (joke above) who wouldn't necessarily vote for the full and speedy recovery.

In any case, many of the people I met while I was a *rebbetzin* were not relating to me but rather through me. Sometimes, I was simply invisible. I recall many an engagement where Jack and I would arrive as guests to a congregant's home and the call would go out, "The rabbi's here!" One thing is for sure: People made assumptions about who I was based on whom I was married to.

I remember one of my "*rebbetzin*" experiences in New Jersey. Jack and I had been there maybe a month and it was the fall harvest holiday of *Sukkot*—that one where you build those little huts. The evening celebration in the *sukkah* was over and I was helping a few of the women clean up. They were speaking with each other in that familiar way of people in a small town who have grown up knowing each other's business. One woman was recalling another's "wild days" until she realized I was in the room. At that moment, her hand went up to her mouth and she whispered, with a touch of fear, "Oh no! The *rebbetzin!*" "Oh my God." I thought, *Are they actually worried about revealing themselves to me?* "Come on, girls." I responded, "You don't know the first thing about me."

This scene would be repeated time and time again during the fifteen years I was married to Jack. Over and over, people would feel the need to be prim and proper around me and to make assumptions about who I was because of who I was married to. For many, they so strongly wanted me to be the image of who they thought a rabbi's wife should be that there was nothing I could say that would change that. Some put me on a pedestal and others made me invisible. The few who heard me and could set aside their assumptions became my intimate friends.

One-Way Intimacy
A Note About Narcissism

Whoever loves becomes humble. Those who love have,
so to speak, pawned a part of their narcissism.

~ Sigmund Freud, neurologist and psychiatrist

THE MOST DIRECT ROAD TO ONE-WAY INTIMACY with real human-flesh people is through narcissism. I am not talking about run of the mill "What about me?" "What's in it for me?" self-centeredness that too many of us have most of the time, and all of us ought to have some of the time. I'm talking about the clinically diagnosable I-can't-relate-to-something-if-it-isn't-part-of-my-own-experience kind of narcissism that unfortunately entraps some of the more wounded individuals in our society. If they are cold, you must be cold; if they didn't see it, it didn't happen; if it's not important to them, it can't possibly be important.

Here's the problem: When someone is narcissistic, the only kind of intimacy they can have is the kind that is centered around their experience or their agenda. They can only really know, see, or understand you if it relates to them. It doesn't mean they can't have intimate experiences; it means that opportunities for intimate moments with narcissists are limited.

Some professions and lifestyles lend themselves to narcissism. For example, performers can be narcissistic. They have a kind of intimacy with the audience and their groupies that definitely fulfills a kind of intimacy need for many. Doctors, lawyers, clergy, coaches, therapists—really any charismatic leader—these are professions where being a narcissist is not necessarily a deterrent to success. Your ailment becomes your doctor's problem to solve, your grandmother's funeral is your clergy's afternoon leadership activity, the coach's and the lawyer's reputations are built on your success on and in the court.

But narcissists do not always do so well in team activities. That collaborative agenda is not always easy for them to integrate. I once had a job that I did joyfully and successfully and then I got a new boss. He was narcissistic and he didn't really know what I was doing. As a result, I could never get my agenda to be on his agenda because he was always laying his agenda on mine. I found that depressing and I can't stand to be depressed for more than a couple of hours, so I quit that job. The trick with narcissists is to figure out how to make your agenda feel like theirs. Then you get them one hundred percent.

Therapy

A psychiatrist is a fellow who asks you a lot of expensive questions your wife asks for nothing.

~ Joey Adams, comedian and author

WHEN JACK AND I GOT DIVORCED, WE BOTH made a commitment to go, on our own, into therapy. We knew that we each had a lot of pent-up emotions and that the one most likely to suffer from that was our son. (By the way, wanting to appear more normal, we don't always tell our friends how amicable our divorce is. Not that we haven't had our moments. Like the time, on our way to breakup couples' counseling, I jumped out of the car at a red light and walked three miles home because I couldn't stand to share airspace with Jack for another moment.)

The therapeutic relationship is a perfect example of what I call limited, albeit powerful, intimacy. The therapist's mission is to create and hold a container for forty-five minutes of the deepest and most focused listening, understanding, and knowing of the other. In those forty-five minutes, the client is encouraged to share with the therapist her deepest and most personal feelings. It is rarely the other way around.

Just because the relationship appears one-way doesn't mean it isn't profound, however. In *Loves' Executioner*, the best-selling collection of case stories by psychiatrist Irvin Yalom, he writes about Carlos, an insensitive, despicable, womanizer who was dying of lymphoma. Under Yalom's guidance, Carlos achieves a degree of authenticity and open-heartedness facing his death that he never before approached during his otherwise misdirected existence. He's so grateful that, on his deathbed, he squeezes Yalom's hand and whispers, "Thank you for saving my life."

On one level, therapy may appear to be one-way, but that is only by one measure. Dig a little deeper and we find an exchange of significant consequence.

Charismatic Intimacy

*The easiest kind of relationship
is with ten thousand people,
the hardest is with one.*

~ Joan Baez, folk singer, songwriter, social activist

CHARISMA IS A POWER THING. MY DASHBOARD dictionary defines charisma as a "compelling attractiveness or charm that can inspire devotion in others." People who have charisma have a gift to make people feel. They speak or sing or write and, in so doing, express a deep collective feeling better and stronger than any of us could express ourselves. They unite us to say, "Yes! That's how I feel!" They know us without knowing our names and we feel that we know them.

There is mounting evidence that even these virtual intimate relationships can contribute to our health and well-being. I like thinking that the angels are involved—that these charismatic folks are in some way a little closer to the angels and that the conversations or art they are manifesting is one of the ways in which the angels interact with our human experience. I can think of lots of examples. One that comes to mind is Oprah.

I have never met Oprah Winfrey, yet I feel I know her. I hardly watch TV and have to confess that I have seen her show only a couple of times. She has such a strong, ubiquitous presence, however, that she can be known beyond her TV show. I know that she is smart, because I see how she has so intelligently built her business world. I know that she is courageous because I have read how she has helped countless women deal with their experiences of abuse thanks to her willingness to reveal and deal with her own. I know that she has the integrity that we wish all our public figures possessed because I read about her response to her experience with

James Frey. I know that she cares deeply about more than just herself because I watched how she built a school in South Africa and adopted hundreds of emerging young women leaders as her family.

On the one hand, this is a One-Way Intimacy. I can know Oprah because of how much she is willing to reveal in public, but that knowing isn't going to be reciprocated. We're not going to take a walk, or have lunch, or invite each other over for slumber parties. When I get that contract or David wins that writing contest, I'm not going to be calling Oprah. When she hits a bump in her road, it isn't going to be me she comes to for empathy and creative problem-solving. This knowing with celebrities is really a one-way thing. Or is it?

Although we have never met, in some way I do feel known by Oprah. Although she doesn't know my name or my specific story, I can't help but feel that on a higher level she knows me very well. I remember once being in the audience where two religious leaders from different traditions were on stage having a private and intimate conversation. As each one shared his truths with the other, we were drawn into the conversation as if it were our own. Halfway through the evening, one of the leaders turned to those of us in the audience and said, "It's almost like it's not us talking, but rather the angels beyond us who needed to have this conversation."

That's what this Charismatic Intimacy feels like to me. It's not just Oprah tuning into and strengthening our culture by strengthening women's culture, just like it wasn't just Martin Luther King Jr. exploding the vision of equality or just Jack Gabriel singing about the need to bless good choices. It feels like an activity at a higher vibration and a place where we are more simply and permeably connected. Like a freshly resined bow, it plays us like a violin.

Empathy

*Honoring the simple reality of another person's experience
is an instant link to the bigger world outside one's self.
It's the seed of empathy, and it's free.*

~ The Big Moo, Seth Godin, editor

THERE ARE MANY PEOPLE WHO, FOR ME, exemplify intimacy with ideas: Ken Wilbur and his Integral Theory of Everything; Barbara Kingsolver and her writing that expresses deep ecology. Another person who has profoundly influenced the educational system with his intimate ideas is Howard Gardner.

Howard Gardner is a professor of education at Harvard University, who, in 1983, developed the theory of Multiple Intelligences*. Basically, he says that the way we have framed intelligence up until recently—for example, I.Q. testing—is way too limited. It's kind of like the same argument I am making about the words we use to describe intimate connections. Too limited. He suggests that we look at ten broad categories of competencies and recognize that students have different levels of intelligence in each. So, for example, a child who may not be able to solve quadratic equations with ease may be the best one to help classmates resolve conflict.

This theory has really taken off and we find thousands of educators applying his ideas in their classrooms. As the educators gain an intimate relationship with the idea of multiple intelligences,

---

* Gardner's intelligences are: Verbal/Linguistic intelligence; Logical-mathematical intelligence; Visual/Spatial intelligence; Bodily-Kinesthetic intelligence; Musical/Rhythmic intelligence; Interpersonal intelligence; Intrapersonal intelligence; Environmental/Naturalist intelligence; Existential intelligence; Spiritual intelligence

many recognize its truth as it speaks more authentically to their personal and professional experiences in education. The more intimate a relationship the educator has with the idea of Multiple Intelligences, the luckier the students in the class are.

My son is really lucky because his school formally recognizes Gardner's contribution and actively uses it in the development of curriculum. In fact, they've taken it even further. They are part of the IB Primary Years program. That means that in addition to applying Gardner's intelligences in curriculum planning, they also focus on the process of learning through eight concepts[*] and integrate the teaching of ten human characteristics[†].

The teachers need to be intimate with these ideas in order for any of this education to be effective. Here's an example of how they do it.

When David was in third grade, he had a weekly homework assignment called "Country Connections." Each Monday the students chose a country. They then had to conduct research on the Internet to find a current event from that country. (Basically, they just needed to Google the nation and the news articles related to it came up at the top.) The assignment was to write a few sentences responding to that current event as if they were a student of the same grade and age in that country. They chose their responses based on the list of characteristics above and also from a list of attitudes. The students didn't have to write volumes. They wrote just two sentences using a characteristic and two sentences using an attitude.

In David's first week, he picked "Guinea-Bissau." Have you ever hard of Guinea-Bissau? I hadn't either. Turns out it is a little West

---

[*] The eight concepts are: Form (What is it like?); Function (How does it work?); Causation (Why is it like this?); Change (How is it changing?); Connection (How is it connected to other things?); Perspective (What are the points of view?); Responsibility (What is our responsibility?); Reflection (How do we know?)

[†] The IB list of ten characteristics includes: Inquirers; Thinkers; Communicators; Risk-Takers; Knowledgeable; Principled; Caring; Open-Minded; Well-Balanced; Reflective

African country—one of the ten poorest countries in the world. The current event David found was that the President-elect of the country had just returned from a six-nation African tour, where he talked about the crisis in his country because his opponent didn't want to admit defeat.

From the list of characteristics, David picked "principled" and he wrote, "The guy who lost should just give up. He should just admit that the guy who won, really won." Then the attitude he picked was "confidence" and he wrote, "I have confidence that the new guy will be able to carry on." Oh, I almost forgot. The final piece of the assignment was that each student made a two- to three-minute presentation about their story every Wednesday.

Research. Geography. Current Events. Writing. Public Speaking. All of these subjects are stimulated in this assignment. But if you ask the teacher about the purpose of the assignment, do you know what he says? The main educational purpose of the assignment is empathy—that David, for a moment, put himself in the place of another and imagine the experience of the other. At eight years old, David was learning to be a citizen of the world. What more could one ask of education?

Checking In

*What man actually needs is not a tensionless state
but rather the striving and struggling for some goal worthy
of him. What he needs is not the discharge of tension
at any cost, but the call of a potential meaning
waiting to be fulfilled by him.*

~ Viktor Frankl, neurologist, psychiatrist,
author, Holocaust survivor

IN COSTA RICA, THE CULTURE IS NOT ANYWHERE near as different from my own as it is in, say, Japan. At times, it is more formal in Costa Rica, and the attitude toward use of resources is different. But I know that both these things are, to different degrees, part of the history of my American culture.

Nevertheless, a number of opportunities for personal and cultural introspection surfaced while we were there. For example, the use of resources. The year before our first visit, the metal frame of David's eyeglasses had broken right at the bridge. I took them back to the place of purchase and they told me there was nothing they could do to fix it. We spent $180 to replace them. One year later, in Costa Rica, David was getting dressed and tripped while pulling on his pants. He fell over and smashed his face on the floor and the lens fell out as the frame once again broke at the bridge. Our host family suggested we take it to the jeweler who kept it for a day, soldered the broken joint and returned it to us looking like new. He charged us $1.75.

Another opportunity for introspection was experiencing the variety of parenting styles in this large host family of ours, and reflecting on my own. Just as in any community, each family parents somewhat differently. In some families, parents are obsessed with their children's education, working side by side with them for hours every day. Others hardly supervise their children at all.

Some children seem to be free to play wherever they please, while others are not allowed outside an invisible bubble around their house. There is, however, one thing about my parenting style that had vexed them all.

One Sunday, we went with a couple of car-loads of the family to a nearby public park that had a 360-degree view of the region. There, as had happened more than a few times every day, David came over to me to ask if he could eat a little piece of candy that one of the children had given to him.

It has always been our custom for David to ask me if he can have candy offered to him. In the Republic of Boulder, one of the most politically correct cities on earth, it is the custom for parents to highly supervise the sugar consumption of young people. In Costa Rica, the candy thing is so pervasive that I was pretty busy trying to keep up with this duty. In every corner store, penny candy (remember that? bins of candy for a penny each!) is readily available. It is common for children to make a once-or-twice daily trip to pick up a small bag of penny candy. Then, throughout the day, they give it to each other. This had resulted in David running—sometimes from three houses down—as many as four or five times a day to ask if he could eat a little piece of candy. Unless it was right before a meal, I usually, often with a sigh of resignation, said yes.

On that particular Sunday, when David came running with candy in hand, all the grown-ups looked at me incredulously. I think they imagined they hadn't heard correctly. Was David actually asking for my permission to eat this little piece of candy? This type of supervision, in Costa Rica, is completely unheard of.

As their mouths hung open, I explained to them about Boulder, about how all my friends and all of the moms and dads of David's friends endure this "Can I eat this?" question throughout the day. Their mouths remained open so long that I had to ask myself "Why am I doing this?" In Boulder, I never had the thought to ask myself this question. Among some of my circles, I am the lenient mom in the area of sugar consumption. I have my rules—not in the morning and not just before a meal. I don't send it to school and I usually do not allow it more than once a day. Suddenly, however, this watchdog mentality felt so controlling that I had to look at it.

Now, we are not talking about a 250-300 calorie candy bar five times a day. What we are talking about are little lifesaver/jolly rancher/saltwater taffy-type candies. What are they? 10, 20 calories apiece? That's less sugar than most people use in their coffee. And the whole idea of children sharing with each other—there is a learned generosity and gratitude in that that is beautiful to watch. If you could have seen David's face when I would say "yes" to one of these little "*confites*," you'd know something deeper about God's joy. Needless to say, David was in candy heaven.

But there remained the question, for me, of control. I gave it lots of thought, weighing the short- and long-term consequences of an increase in David's level of sugar consumption versus the short- and long-term consequences of my controlling David's candy consumption to such a degree. I considered the level of joy when I said "yes" versus my not being in the conversation at all. At that moment, it felt like the emotional consequences of my control of David's sugar consumption were heavier than the physical consequences of the sugar.

So, we tried something new. David did not need to ask my permission to eat these little pieces of candy that were offered to him—as long as he knew the person who proffered them. If he had a yearning for a piece of candy, and it was not just before a meal, we'd go buy enough pieces to share with all the kids. I tried my best to get the "edge" out of my voice—not to be annoyed or judgmental of David's desire for sugar. It appears to be a very natural desire of all young people. Therefore, he ought not feel any shame about it.

Since the discovery of sugar beets and sugar cane, humans have been enjoying sweet things. I have come to the conclusion that these little candies are not inherently bad like drugs or alcohol, and as long as kids eat healthy meals and also eat fresh fruits and brush their teeth, I am not convinced there is any harm. I might even think it's simply fine.

The experiment got mixed reviews from both of us. I missed seeing the joy radiating in David's being when I say "yes" and David said he did, too. I guess there was an intimacy in the exchange—a touchpoint and a way for David to connect with me in this foreign land. At the same time, it provided a chance for me to witness his experience, his joy that he was getting to eat candy. Perhaps we needed to find another way—one that promotes the connection, honors the witnessing and, at the same time, loosens the reigns.

Madeline Levine, the author of *The Price of Privilege*, calls us well-educated, well-intentioned parents to task. She says that with our over-protective and micromanaging ways we are depriving our children of the experience of getting to know themselves. I thank my Costa Rican family for putting the speed bump in the road so that I had a chance to reflect. Sometimes we need to go 2,500 miles from home to learn a lesson. Who would have ever thought that it would take traveling a half a continent away for me to re-examine, and ultimately alter, my position on something as small and sweet as a piece of candy?

Tribal Intimacy

Though I am different from you,
we were born involved in one another.

~ White-Horse Tibetan Saying

WHEN JACK AND I FIRST MOVED TO Colorado, we traveled around the region quite a bit. There was one year early on during which some friends of ours in Oregon organized a trip for rabbis and their beloveds for the first week after the autumn high holidays. For a rabbi, the Jewish High Holidays are like a marathon—nineteen events over a six-week period, combined with courting new members and the start of the religious school year. You can imagine how burned out those poor rabbis are during that time. Consider nineteen events over a period of six weeks, and burned out is an understatement.

Our friends had a friend who had organized a tour for photographers to Canyon De Chelles, near where Arizona, New Mexico, Colorado, and Utah meet to make the four corners. That trip had included a stay with a Navajo family and hiking around the area as the photography-learning classroom. Our friends decided to organize a similar trip for rabbis and their partners at the end of the six-week push.

It proved quite an experience. We were a group of about twenty who came from all over the country. We arrived an hour before Shabbat began on a Friday. We camped on the land of a Navajo family—Chauncey and Daniel, a father-and-son duo. Over the next few days, we experienced a cultural exchange that was renewing for all involved. Our relationship with each Navajo we met changed when they realized we were not Christians. Christians have a bit of a bad reputation among the Navajo given their history for persecuting more than a couple generations of Navajo. It seems that during the Frontier days, Christians separated families, put children in boarding schools, and hit them if they tried to use any language other than English. Did you see the movie *Rabbit Fence*? It was a beautiful and moving film that portrayed just the story we heard over and over again from the Navajos.

At first, I didn't get that they didn't get it, because they just assumed all white Americans were Christians and that all Christians were related to those who had oppressed them. One morning, while I was taking a break from the morning service, Chauncey, who must have been around seventy and was missing many teeth, joined me as I stood yards away. I was taking in the incredible landscape—vast clay-colored walls of the canyon shooting upwards—with our group below, all of us swathed in colorful prayer shawls as we danced with an old Torah scroll.

He said, "What kind of celebration is this?"

"It is how Jews celebrate the Sabbath," I said.

"What are Jews?" he asked.

Now, having lived in Colorado for a few years, I had met plenty of people who had never met a Jewish person before. But never before had I met an American who didn't know about the Jews. I tried to figure out if he knew anything about Hitler and the Holocaust. No, nothing. So, I simply told him that we are a tribal people who had been around a long time. We too had been persecuted by White people, I emphasized. Although small in number, we held on tightly to our tradition. He got that. So, eventually, did the others.

There was one woman in particular whose whole presence with us shifted when she understood that we were also a tribal people. She was a medicine woman, around sixty years old. She shared many stories with us, including how it hurt her cheeks to speak in English because the muscles in her face had developed while speaking Navajo. She told us how her people are one with everything, that when they build their houses they apologize to the spiders that need to move. She rubbed the dirt onto her arms and her legs, showing us how her skin is the same color as the land.

She talked about how when women stop menstruating, that is really when they come into their power. She alluded to customs for young women when they begin to menstruate. That piqued our interest because in the Jewish tradition, customs for women have been lost. While we have renewed the practices of woman who gather for *Rosh Chodesh* and Croning (after sixty years of age), we haven't yet figured out what to do for girls as they become women. The Bat Mitzvah doesn't quite make it.

At first, the Navajo woman was completely reluctant to share with us. It was only after she had shared with us stories of how the Christian schools would not allow days off for their rituals and we shared with her our stories of how sometimes our children had exams scheduled on our holidays that she got it. There was a moment where her head twitched and her face relaxed, and then she opened up in a whole new way.

Sometimes intimacy is slow in coming, but when it arrives it can cross even the widest chasms.

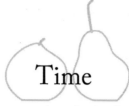

Time

*How we spend our days is, of course,
how we spend our lives.*

~ Annie Dillard, author

I AM COMMITTED TO NOT BEING OVERWHELMED in my life, and for the most part, I am successful. I plan my days to accomplish a good amount and I still make time to sit down with David at breakfast and dinner—with enough leisure time to luxuriate in sports, hip-hop and video-game talk. When I pick him up from school, I do not whisk him away. Rather, I let him play for a really long time on the playground. Sometimes we end up walking some of the other kids home so their parents—who are anxious to leave—can go, but the kids can stay. I hardly ever plan anything after school.

I remember when David was three a friend was doing me favor. I had an appointment and she agreed to take David with her and her two kids for the afternoon. They had a soccer game to get to and as David was putting on his shoes, she said, "Hurry up, we're running late." David looked up, confused, and I realized that in the three years of his life, he had never heard anyone say, "Hurry up!"

In those first three years, life for David was at David's pace. As the only child of a mom who worked from home, we never had to rush off to a sibling's game or get to childcare so I could get to work. Childcare would arrive and for David, it was just another adoring person who had come to play with him.

When he and I (or the adoring childcare provider) would walk in the neighborhood, it was at the speed of toddler. If David wanted to stop and look at the weeds growing in the cracks in the sidewalk, we'd stop and look until he was done.

Although "we gotta go" is now a common phrase in the house, we still maintain a very sane schedule. But I feel I am alone in this regard. I am surrounded by people who are rushing from one meeting/job/kids/ activity to another. They don't think they can be away from their e-mail for more than a day. They rarely sit down to a meal with friends and family. In fact, if they had a chunk of free time, they wouldn't know what to do with themselves. While they feel stressed and exhausted by this pace of life, they still think it's okay. They have lost their sense of personal time. They have lost the ability to luxuriate in anything. They have lost their knowledge of self.

Boys and Their Toys

'I'd rather play inside.
That's where all the electrical outlets are.'

~ Richard Louv, author of *Last Child in*
the Woods, quoting a 4th grader

I GREW UP IN A LOW TESTOSTERONE HOME. I AM the youngest of three sisters and the sports page was the only section of the paper my father did *not* read. Each of my sisters has one child—both girls. When my son was born, we all looked at each other like "Now, what do we do?"

Fortunately for me, that year and during the couple of years that followed, a plethora of new books on boys debuted—*The Wonder of Boys* (Gurian), *Real Boys* (Pollack), *Raising a Son* (Elium), and *Raising Cain* (Kindlon, Thompson). I bought all of them, and I read all of them. I was bound and determined to get a handle on what being a boy was all about.

The first real test of that vow came the summer after David turned four. We were at the Boulder Creek Festival, where the "Renaissance Adventure Camp" had a booth. It was more than a booth, really. They had a cordoned-off area where people paid two dollars to enter and battle each other with padded swords. Up until then, we were a sword-free, gun-free household, and our TV watching consisted of musicals that I had taken out of the library. I don't think David had ever seen anything quite like it, and it drew him in. Quite frankly, he was mesmerized.

"Mommy, can we play?" I didn't want to hear it. Spend four bucks knowing that after ten minutes I'd have had more than enough. I am a pacifist and I couldn't imagine myself poking my son with a sword. I said, "No, sweetie, I'm sorry." I made to go, but David didn't leave that spot. Then I heard the man in charge giving instructions to some older boys on their way in.

"No head, no face, no neck, and no private parts," he said, adding, "Anyone is fair game." I looked around. While there were a few parents in the ring, there were plenty of kids in there by themselves. I watched a little longer and no one was too rough, really. And everyone did seem to be having so much fun. Could I actually send my son in there and not have to go myself? Could I, should I let him explore the primal, archetypal urges to be a hero and slay the dragon? Would I have to watch?

I paid the two dollars and in went David. After about ten minutes he came back over to the front and I thought he was done, but no, he was just trading in the puny little sword he had first picked up for a bigger one. After another twenty minutes or so, I borrowed a chair from one of the nearby vendors and had a seat in the shade. After about an hour, I approached Aaron, the man in charge, to inquire about camps. "What you really need to be running," I said to him, "is a program for pacifist mothers who have trouble with their boys playing with swords."

That was Aaron's segue. He is a martial artist and practices offensive, defensive, and contemplative martial arts. He spoke with me about how boys think the power is here (making a fist) but how it is really here (bringing his fist to his heart). It was beautiful. I watched more deeply and saw an older boy, maybe sixteen, who had gotten down on his knees to be more at David's level, say to my son, "Hey, bud. Show me what you've got," while he firmly, yet gently, dare I say, intimately battled with my boy. David was totally in the flow. I decided to let him go as long as he wanted.

Two and half hours later he was tiring. Although he didn't stop on his own, he didn't put up a struggle either when I said it was time to go. I had never seen him so deeply satisfied. It was a profound experience for both of us. For David, it was the real beginning of manhood, and for me, it was the commencement of letting go of the little child. We bought a couple of swords and had an important conversation about guns and weapons, with a focus on how different they are (guns are violent; attackers are often very distant and can hide, versus swords, which bring you face-to-face to engage with your opponent and can be used with skill and grace).

There would be more moments, albeit less profound, for us as I, a single mother, would attempt to navigate the world of boys.

I recall one time when David was in kindergarten. He was sitting with a stack of cards across the table from a friend, the two of them playing their own version of "mine's bigger than yours."

"I have more cards than you do," said one. "No, I have more than you," said the other. My impulse was to say, "Boys, it doesn't matter who has more," but by then I already knew better. To them, it did matter, very much, and if I were to say it didn't ... well, at that age, they'd be processing, "My mommy knows everything, so she must be right, so my feelings must be wrong, and maybe I can't trust my feelings." We mothers have to be careful not to impose our feminist ways onto our sons, especially as they are trying to figure out who they are.

The last big rule that dropped was around video games. When David was very young, I had read in one of those boy books about the development of the brain and that up to the age of ten, excessive time in front of a screen can retard brain development. So I had made a proclamation early on that we would not have any video games in the house until David was ten.

Ha!

I did hold out pretty long, but when David got to second grade, he came home saying, "Everyone has one." While I am not ordinarily drawn into that kind of reasoning, I did examine the situation. Indeed, every boy in his class had some kind of video-game apparatus. Even the one family who was usually more concerned about these things than I was—even their boys had GameBoys for long car trips. David always wanted to go to others kids' houses to play (and then only wanted to play video games) and there were kids who didn't want to come over to our house because we lacked such entertainment. Like the question of candy in Costa Rica, I carefully weighed the consequences of adherence to my proclamation. In the end, I decided that the social cost was higher than the brain-development payoff. I mean, what's a few IQ points, anyway? We borrowed an old Super Nintendo from David's godmother, and I let go.

But I didn't stop thinking about it. The scholar/practitioner in me continued to ask, "Is this nature or nurture? Is David drawn to this because his friends are doing it? Why is it almost exclusively boys? Is it the way the products are marketed? What is going on in the brain that hooks them so?" I also looked at the intimacy with which the boys connect over these games.

It's not just in America, either, I can tell you that. On our most recent trip to Costa Rica, it was a little out of control. Playing video games was the first things all the boys there wanted to do. Those with enough resources have their own systems, and those who don't can pay about a dollar an hour to sit on someone's porch and play. Parents there are having the same conversations we are here. How much is too much? While the boys are bonding with Crash Bandicoot, the parents are bonding over what to do.

I had an hour-long discussion about it in Spanish with my friends Félix and Rocio as David played with their son Júlian. Elena (Estefano and Gaston's mom—they have a Playstation) and I had a funny moment at the end of our three weeks when I said to her (in Spanish), "Ordinarily, I don't let David play every day, but since your boys were playing, I let it be." She laughed and responded (in Spanish), "I ordinarily don't let them play except when they are on vacation, but I figured since David is here and he is allowed to play …."

But Costa Rica really is a middle-class country, so I couldn't draw any conclusions about the nature/nurture, cultural-marketing questions from this experience alone. Then I saw the movie *The Weeping Camel* and I understood the universality of the draw of "The Screen."

The movie is a documentary that was a hit due to sheer serendipity. While filming the lives of a family of herders in Mongolia's Gobi region, the filmmakers unexpectedly came upon a drama when a mother camel rejected her newborn albino calf. Camels are critical to these herders' lives and this was therefore a crisis. We, the viewers, are treated with a magical window into the lives of this small family as they problem solve how to get the mother to care for her offspring. Two brief moments in the movie brought home "The Screen's" universal appeal.

After many stalled attempts to get the mother to feed her calf, toward the end of the movie, a teenage boy is sent to the nearest village (a few days' travel away) in order to find someone who ultimately resolves the crisis. His younger cousin, who is maybe six years old, begs and is finally allowed to accompany his teenage cousin on this journey. It is evidently the younger boy's first trip away from his extremely isolated lifestyle.

The duo's first stop is for a meal and an overnight stay with acquaintances along the way. This family has a satellite dish and a TV inside their yurt. The young boy is sitting with a plate of food in front of him, fork stuck in midair, with his mouth hanging open as he stares at what is obviously his first encounter with "The Screen." The hostess says to him, "Eat your dinner!"

In the next scene we watch the boys as they enter the village and buy some batteries in a store—and probably some other supplies—before they head over to the school to find the problem solver. When they ultimately return to the family, the little boy is telling his father about his adventure to the village. What did he like best, his father asks? The boy answers (in Mongolian dialect with English subtitles), "Dad, they have this game …" as he holds his hands close together and moves his thumbs as if he were playing with a joystick. I kid you not, this is for real.

I am left with a myriad of questions: How is it that a boy from the desert, isolated from marketing campaigns and peer influence, finds video games so attractive? What is it about video games that speak so deeply to the soul of a boy? Is it filling a void? Or has it touched on something deeply embedded is the male psyche? Is this an important part of a boy's journey to manhood? As a mother, what is my role in relationship to these games? How and where do I draw the lines? Is it any of my business? Is it incumbent upon reflective men to guide the boys through the quagmire of electronic toys?

Although each question leads to more questions, one thing is certain: Video game intimacy among boys is alive and well all over the Earth.

The Biggest Challenge
(formerly titled Automobiles, Technology and the Death of Public Conversation)

Once, when repaving work emptied the street for a
couple of days, the atmosphere transformed. People lingered
on the sidewalks and fell into conversation with strangers.
I met two of my neighbours for the first time that week....
Studies around the world show a direct correlation
between cars and community: the less traffic that flows
through an area, and the more slowly it flows, the more
social contact among the residents.

~ Carl Honoré, author of *In Praise of Slowness*

FOR THE LAST EIGHTEEN MONTHS, I HAVE LIVED near a state park. Yesterday was a glorious fall day, David was with his dad, and I had just bought a new pair of walking shoes. So I got myself to the park, entered the Wetlands Preserve Trail and walked for forty-five minutes. It was glorious. What I can't believe is that I've been to this park only four times in the past year and a half!

While I was driving home, I pondered why it's so hard for me to visit the park and I realized it's the drive. It's not the length of time—it only takes four minutes—but rather the road itself. In that four minutes, I have to cross through a huge, god-awful, non-human-scale intersection that is bordered by strip malls and parking garages, pass under a figure-eight interstate interchange with six lanes feeding off it, and then drive on an eight-lane highway in order to get to the entrance of the park.

It reminds me of an experience I had a few years ago in Asheville, North Carolina. I was on a mission to explore the cohousing* communities in North Carolina for a possible reloca-tion. Our first stop was Asheville.

I had heard wonderful things about Asheville—small town with lots of culture, near the mountains, and a socially-conscious feel. We connected with the cohousing folks there and also met with a few like-minded members of the Jewish community. We loved the town square with its music and food. Although much of it felt right, something was off.

It was the roads. Asheville is framed by three highways—really more trisected than framed. Okay, maybe scarred is a better word. It is nearly impossible to travel on slow roads in Asheville, and for every destination, we were told which exit to take. Even to go just down the road a bit meant an entrance and exit ramp. By the end of three days, I'd had enough of the highways and told my family, "I can't live here."

One of the things I loved best about being in Costa Rica was that there were only a few roads in town and most people walked everywhere. Public eye contact was a normal part of every day. In contrast, my drive to the state park felt like a trip to the moon.

What happened that caused such a dramatic shift in our lives, where we are losing the opportunity to know where it is that we truly live? I believe it all started with the automobile, or more accu-rately when the automobile became enclosed and could travel more than ten miles an hour. "Everyone move over, I'm coming through" was likely the genesis of our narcissistic culture. If it is outside my bubble, it doesn't concern me.

While the automobile may have been the beginning, it, alone, isn't to blame, because…along came television.

Television has become *the major* mode of entertainment. Robert Putnam, in *Bowling Alone*, devotes a chapter to Technology and

---

*From the Cohousing.org website: "Cohousing is a type of collaborative housing in which residents actively participate in the design and operation of their own neighborhoods. Cohousing residents are consciously committed to living as a community. The physical design encourages both social contact and individual space."

Mass Media. He is meticulous with the data and there are so much that it is difficult to choose just a few representative examples. Here's my best try...

"Between 1965 and 1995, we gained an average of six hours a week of leisure time, and we spent almost all six of those additional hours watching TV." In fact 40 percent of our all our leisure time (in 1995) was spent watching TV.*

"Time diaries show that husbands and wives spend three or four times as much time watching television together as they spend talking to each other and six to seven times as much as in community activities outside home."

"People who say that TV is their "primary form of entertainment" volunteer and work on community projects less often, attend fewer dinner parties and fewer club meetings, spend less time visiting friends, entertain at home less, picnic less, are less interested in politics, give blood less often, write friends less regularly, make fewer long distance calls, send fewer greeting cards and less e-mail, and express more road rage than demographically matched people who differ only in saying that TV is *not* their primary form of entertainment."

"Nothing—not low education, not full-time work, not long commutes in urban agglomerations, not poverty or financial distress—is more broadly associated with civic disengagement and social disconnection than is dependence on television for entertainment."

Putnam continues, quoting political communications specialist Roderick Hart who says that TV viewing can lead to a kind of "remote control politics," in which viewers feel engaged without being engaged." Like junk food, TV, especially TV entertainment, satisfies craving without real nourishment.

Putnam shares with us another remarkable fact: While it took sixty-seven years from the introduction of the telephone (1890) until seventy-five percent of the American public was using that

---

* With increases in Internet uses in the last decade, I'll bet that cumulative "screen time" is even higher.

tool, and 52 years from the introduction of the automobile (1908) until 75% of American households had one, television (1948) achieved this same penetration in seven years.

Of course, television viewing has morphed into screens of all kinds of activities—Internet surfing, video games, shopping online, e-mail addiction. The speed of viewing has also increased at an inhuman pace. A few months ago, David invited me to watch a video of a concert tour of one of his favorite bands. Wanting to share that experience with him, I enthusiastically sat on the couch. But shortly after we started watching it, I felt sick—literally. The movement between shots (more than one shot per second?) made me dizzy. I really wanted to watch, to see the artists and to know them not just by their music but also by their presence. I wanted to see their faces with the fullness of their expression. I wanted to know what they were feeling by watching the energy that comes through their eyes. And because of the jumping from stage to audience to close-up to band shot—all in a matter of seconds—I got nothing but nauseated.

I have a similar reaction when I see the TV shows David watches. I have no quarrel with the content of *Ned's Declassified* or *That's So Raven*, but the visual stimulation overwhelms me. I don't mean to point fingers, but I think it all started with *Sesame Street* and their effort to keep kids' attention. As they got older, MTV joined the fray. Somehow we got it into our heads that faster is better and that more stimulation is a good thing. Guess what? We were wrong. It's not, and we don't know how to stop it. And the cost is high. "Just leave me alone in front of my screens," we say. We are losing the ability to reflect.

So we have the automobiles, the television and various other screens. And, as if that weren't enough, then came the cell phone.

While researching the history of the cell phone, I learned that when Martin Cooper made the first cell phone call on April 3, 1973, it caused a fundamental technology and communications market shift toward the person and away from the place. Similar to the automobile, the potential of another insulating, personal bubble appeared around us.

Today, there are more cellular subscribers than land-line phone subscribers in the world. In the United Kingdom, there are more mobile phones than people in the country. The Gartner Group predicts that one billion mobile phones will be sold worldwide in the year 2009.[*]

I recently took David to Steamboat Springs. We arrived late Wednesday night and went into town for dinner. As luck would have it, the first place we found had both *fettuccine alfredo* (David's favorite) and a pool table. Pool is one of the ways David and I connect these days. After a satisfying meal and a couple games of pool, we headed out the door—but oh! my way is blocked. There is a woman on the phone and she has just reached the party at the other end of the line. She has stopped right in the doorway to carry out her conversation. There is no other way out and no way to get around her. "Excuse me," I say gently. She doesn't hear me. "Excuse Me!'" I say a little louder. "Oh, sorry," she says, as she moves down the steps. It was genuine; she really was sorry. She was just in her own little world.

Then off we went to the grocery store to buy some staples for the next few days. On our way out, there was a woman on her cell phone blocking the wide pathway out. I do the same "excuse me" routine and eventually—still talking—she moves over, but this time without eye contact and no "I'm sorry."

If it is outside my bubble, it doesn't exist.

In 1998, as part of a Ph.D. dissertation at Harvard, Tay Keong Tan, an ethnographer, asked a member of the Amish community how they know whether or not to admit a new technological invention into their lives. The response was simple. "We can almost always tell if a change will bring good or bad tidings. Certain things we definitely do not want, like the television and the radio. They

---

[*] India's cellular subscriber base rose to 12.6 million in March 2003. India's cell phone users are expected to reach 250 million by 2007. Other interesting statistics: Data from the Ministry of Information Industry show that in China, there are 829 million phone users, 461 million of which used mobile phones while 368 million were fixed-line phone users. They are adding about 1.5 million cell phone subscribers every month.

would destroy our visiting practices. We would stay at home with the television or radio rather then meet with other people. How can we care for the neighbor if we do not visit them or know what is going on in their lives?"

I recently saw an ad, promoting the "benefits" of a high tech minivan. It simultaneously said, "Nothing connects your family like the All-New [brand name minivan]," and "6-hour trip to Grandma's and never heard a peep out of them!" The picture shows each family member with headphones on, each with their own entertainment system. How could the family be connecting if they are not interacting with each other? As Margaret Mead said, "Having two bathrooms ruined the capacity to cooperate." On college campuses, students no longer engage in public conversation between classes. That's because most of them have iPod earbuds in their ears, insulating them from public conversation.

Of this, Robert Putnam reflects, "Our growing social-capital deficit threatens educational performance, safe neighborhoods, equitable tax collection, democratic responsiveness, everyday honesty, and even our health and happiness." Edward Hallowell, M.D., the ADD expert and author of *Driven to Distraction* and *Crazy Busy*, says, "Too much electronic time and not enough human moments lead us to an as yet unnamed medical condition, the symptoms of which are loss of personal vitality, the inability to converse, a craving for screen when separated from one, and low-grade depression.

Uh-oh. We'd better do something.

Union

*The greatest stories are those that resonate our beginnings
and intuit our endings, our mysterious origins and our numinous destinies,
and dissolve them both into one.*

~ Ben Okri, Nigerian author

Floating in the Wilderness

*Those who contemplate the beauty of the Earth find
reserves of strength that will endure as long as life lasts.*

~ Rachel Carson, marine biologist and nature writer

A FEW YEARS AGO, I TREATED MYSELF TO ONE
of those items on my list of "Things To Do Before I Die."
I canoed on the Boundary Waters.

The Boundary Waters Canoe Area Wilderness (BWCAW)
spans 1.3 million acres with 1,200 miles of canoe routes along the
Minnesota border with Canada. It was set aside as a preserve in
1926 and has been maintained in its pristine ways since then.

I had signed up for a "Fall Colors" guided excursion—six days
at the end of September—offered by a small family-owned business, Sawbill Canoe Outfitters in Tofte, Minnesota. It turns out
that I was the only one to sign up, but Dave, the guide, said he
never misses a chance to get out and navigate so he would take me
anyway. So it was just me and Dave, and off we went for six days
on the Boundary Waters.

Now, you may be thinking, it's a little risky to head off into the
wilderness and spend six days with someone you don't know. Not
risky in the sense that any harm would come, but what if the guy's
a jerk? What if you have really different ideas of how to spend the
day? What if your interests and values and politics are offensive to
each other? It could be a vision of hell.

Fortunately, we lucked out. It turns out that Dave, who is about
twenty years my junior, was not only a terrific guide but also an
all-around terrific guy. We had lots to talk about on a variety of
shared-interest subjects—from integrating adventure into a lifestyle to running a small business. I loved hearing his story of how,
at 16, he discovered the wilderness and has been her captive ever

since. I had a deep vicarious pleasure from hearing about Dave's nonprofit organization, Wilderness Classroom. Then there were other moments when I was more of a mentor, sharing some wisdom and lessons learned from my twenty-plus years as a socially conscious entrepreneur. The risk turned out to be a non-issue.

My second concern was about portaging with the canoe. The BWCAW is made up of lots of lakes—both big and small—and in order to get from one to the next, you need to "portage" (i.e., carry the canoe and all your gear). There are lots of rules in the Wilderness Area to keep it wilderness. Only a certain number of permits are given to a limited number of outfitters so that the numbers of people at any given time are small. The campsites are few and far between and there is a strict limit to the number of people allowed at each site, making "partying" non-existent. Canoers are not allowed to pick up driftwood from the shores for firewood. There is no use of any motorized anything, for any reason. There is no signage at all, anywhere.

I applauded all of these rules but one…In the whole of the Wilderness Area you have to carry everything. You can't bring any kind of wheels to roll the canoe or gear over the land when you have to portage. You can't drag the bags or the canoe. That meant multiple trips as we carried all of our belongings (four big packs) and then the canoe. The distance can be as much as a mile for each portage, although we tried to pick a route that kept each one to under a half mile. I wasn't sure my nearly fifty year-old musculoskeletal system was up to it—my back, my knees …. Dave, however, had assured me that it wouldn't be a problem—that he could do it all if necessary. We decided that we would get to a great spot on Day One with all our gear and set up camp there for the duration. Our daily trips would just be with the canoe and one pack.

On that first day—the day with all our stuff—Dave was like a packhorse. On the shorter portages, he would carry the two heaviest packs, one on his front, one on his back. At the same time, he would transport the canoe in his hands with his arms above his shoulders. I'd take the two light packs, one on my front and one on my back. On the longer portages, I'd take one pack and Dave would do the rest, making two trips. In between the portages, we canoed on a half dozen quiet, peaceful lakes before reaching our destination. Two beaver dams, four portages, five lakes, and six hours later, we arrived at our camping spot. We had seen only one other "group" (three people), briefly, along the way.

I was sure I'd be terribly sore from paddling and portaging, but I had not one ache or pain … not even after day three when we paddled all out, for hours, into the wind. It didn't surprise me that I'd somehow avoided the physical discomfort, because I've always believed that I canoed in a past life. That's how I've always understood how being in a canoe makes my soul sing.

The campsite Dave chose was picture perfect—a small inlet for pulling in, a secluded spot for the tent, and an exposed outcropping from which to sit, dine, and view the whole lake. We had decided to pack the heavy canvas tent rather than the lightweight nylon one because the canvas one had a flue that accommodated an "indoor" wood stove. That heating element turned out to be my biggest luxury. Remember, it was September and we were pretty far north. So while the days were pleasant, the nights were chilly and the mornings downright cold. Dave slept outside in a hammock tied between two trees, bundled in his sub-zero bag, while I slept in the tent with my wool cap pulled over my head. In the mornings, when I'd wake up, I'd call out, "Dave, you up yet?" Heeding my call, he'd get out of the hammock, collect a little firewood, come in the tent, start the stove, and set the kettle on for tea. All the while the tent was warming up and the water for morning tea was a-boilin', I was snug in my sleeping bag. Five-star service and a great way to start the day.

What we experienced were five glorious days of quiet near-solitude mixed with a primal use of personal energy as we moved ourselves from lake to lake. We fished for our dinner and pulled our water from the depths of the middle of the lakes. I went skinny-dipping (oh my God!, it was cold), and each day I took some time for writing and reflection. At night, we watched the Northern Lights shimmering like a rainbow, playing hide-and-seek with the black sky. It was Wilderness Intimacy at its best.

Although the whole experience was in the flow, the most intimate wilderness moment occurred one evening when we went for a short paddle at dusk. After a satisfying fire-cooked meal, we set out at a leisurely pace to paddle around the lake. We hadn't seen anyone for days, and other than a few loons, we hadn't witnessed much wildlife either. The ambience defined serenity. The water was still and the sun was setting as we rounded a bend and came through a narrow channel. It was then that time and space stood still. The water was *so* still, in fact, that I was unable to tell where the land ended and the water began. Was it glass?

The gentle dipping of my paddle into the water barely broke the surface and I felt that I was gliding through the air. I had a momentary flash of the Road Runner cartoon where he has run off a cliff and keeps running through the air until he realizes there is no earth beneath him. My heart skipped a beat thinking we might fall. Then I surrendered to the moment. It was magical. Suddenly, I wanted to paint and sing and dance the stillness. I wanted to embrace it, and somehow bottle it. The motionlessness and perfection, the out-of-time and spaceness of it, was intoxicating.

We returned to that spot on our way out of the Boundary Waters so that I could take a photo. When we got there, I didn't recognize it. There was a bit of wind and the water was rippling, and while it was certainly still beautiful, that magic was gone. The moment of intimacy was not to be captured on film, but even now, I can take a deep breath, close my eyes, and for a brief moment feel myself floating in the wilderness.

Belonging

*Friendship is born at that moment
when one person says to another:
'What! You, too? I thought I was the only one.'*

~ C.S. Lewis, author and scholar

W E KNOW THAT INTIMACY IS INHERENT FOR
human survival. We know that infants will die without intimate touch. We know that elders suffer from
depression without intimate connections. Intimacy is like a vita-
min that is necessary for our physical, mental, and spiritual health.
Without it, we are left with a feeling of disconnect—a spiritual
crisis of sorts where we do not feel connected to the people, places,
and things in our daily lives. In this absence of intimate connections, we feel a deficiency and a profound loneliness.

From 1994 through 2005, I was the coordinator and organizer
of a biennial summer conference that brought together more than
800 people for a week-long celebration of Jewish experience. It
is an unusual gathering in that while many Jewish organizations
are designed along denominational lines, this gathering is "post
denominational" by design. The diversity is rich and includes
people who might otherwise be marginalized in traditional Jewish
communities—people born Jewish who have a Buddhist practice,
people estranged from orthodoxy, and those turned off by the
"Judaism Lite" that is offered in some reform communities. It also
includes rabbis, cantors, social activists, teachers, and others who
are actively and joyfully connected to Jewish community.

The learning curve during my first year organizing the event
was as steep as the Andes. There were literally thousands upon
thousands of details to attend to and track: site selection, vendor
relations, fiscal management, content programming, marketing,

publicity, registration, kosher food planning, facilities management, gift shop, healing center, customer service and the recruitment, training, supervision and retention of thirty-five staff/volunteers—all this happening before we welcomed 800 seekers and celebrants into what would be described as a kind of Jewish "Brigadoon." From the outside, it appeared as though my job was all about the details.

I, however, had a different view of my job. It turns out that many of the people who came to the event didn't know anyone else. They had heard about it, it spoke to them on some level, or they knew someone else who had come years before. Many more knew only a few people. I also discovered that for nearly half the people attending, it was their first time. So, while the thousands of details were indeed important, I realized that the most important part of my job was helping people feel that they belonged.

I spoke with the executive director of the organization about how people feel when they are outside the inner circle. He expressed to me that *he* felt outside the inner circle. Curious!? Nearly everyone would consider him in the inner circle, yet he, himself, didn't feel there! The scholar-practitioner in me began to ask questions such as Was this about him? Was this about the organization? Or was it bigger, an existential crisis in America where people don't feel connected?

From that moment on, I made sure that every conference activity was run through the filter of the "new person who doesn't know anyone and is self-conscious about her/his identity." Steeped in kabbalistic tradition, I approached this from a "Four Worlds" perspective, acknowledging that there are always, simultaneously, things happening in the physical, emotional, intellectual, and spiritual realms. It started with how the catalog of classes was presented. It was addressed directly in the "Notes on Living in Community" that was sent in advance. I trained my planning committee of thirty-five people to use the filter in all aspects of their work. The over-arching goal was to create a "container" where everyone felt they could belong.

The scholar-practitioner in me abandoned the registration question about marital status and, instead, asked people about their "intimacy constellations"—questions about how satisfied people were with their relationships in family, work, school, neighborhood, and religious communities. I asked about children living at home or away from home and the need to care for aging parents. I asked about other significant relationships. I asked about hobbies and other passions and how satisfying those activities were. I asked them to identify what kind of affinity group they would want to be a part of at the event with suggestions related to occupation, passions, traumas, and life experiences. The picture of people's lives became rich and deep.

When choosing a site—usually a university setting—the "belonging" theme was put front and center. The connections between and among the classrooms, dining areas, and dorm rooms were of primary importance on the list of requirements. The feel of the place and the spaces where we would gather would make or break the decision. This was the Foundation for belonging.

The Planning Committee—made up of thirty-five creative and committed people who would themselves be participants during the week—was also guided by this principle of belonging. Each member of the Planning Committee was to view herself as collaborating in the creation of a symphony. We paid attention to the subtleties, ridding the composition of distractions by, for example, disabling cable in the dorm rooms and declaring much of the space as cell-free zones. The love and care put into the writing and rehearsal of the score would manifest in each summer's world premier.

The planning could be a little overwhelming, as each person sought to expand and ornament her piece of the whole. The strings shouldn't be too loud throughout performance, nor should the timpani sound too often. At some point in the process—as we approached the end of planning—I would share a little story:

There once was a student of Ikebana (Japanese flower arranging). She had studied the art for many years. She approached her master teacher to say that she felt ready to move to the next level and wanted to publicly show her work in a juried exhibition. Her master gave her three envelopes and told her to go home.

When she got home, she opened the first envelope.

It said, "Take out half the flowers."
She opened the second envelope, and inside it said,
"Take out half the flowers."
She opened the third envelope, and inside it said, "Take out half the flowers."

It was time to rein it in, letting go of some of the brilliant ideas in order to ground what would become our container. With this level of maturity completed, the composer transformed into the conductor—hands up and ready to let the music flow, holding the energy of the entire piece that will begin to unfold—holding the Container for belonging.

Just before the event began, we brought the teachers in for a weekend of togetherness. This pre-session was designed as a perk—a smaller, more intimate setting—where teachers who were being asked to give of themselves to the larger community could, themselves, be nourished. They'd eat, play music, and just hang out together. They'd study a Code of Ethics together to guide their relationships with students. They'd learn together about managing group energy, looking at how to be strong and, at the same time, soft containers where participants could feel both held and propelled into deeper connection with the experience.* The Nourishment for belonging.

As the participants arrived, they were escorted through a "registration process" that was built around the ten *sephirot* of the "Tree of Life," the kabbalistic illustration of the emanations of God,†

---

* The teachers also learned about common pitfalls, for example, when someone removes herself from the group and moves to the back of the room and is talking, the integrity of the container is compromised and the energy leaks. This is a common occurrence. I see it at almost every meeting I attend. Watch it yourself. If you're the one doing it, either move back into the group or leave the room instead of talking in the back.

† The ten *sephirot* (with their loose translations) are: *keter* (union), *chochmah* (wisdom), *binah* (understanding), *chesed* (overflowing loving-kindness), *gevurah* (strength and limits), *tiferet* (Beauty), *netzach* (eternal reverberations), *hod* (gracefulness), *yesod* (foundation, connections between generations), and *malhut* (completion, the great dissolver).

with each *sephira* supporting a part of the process.* This served not only to introduce this important concept to those new to the community, and to bring order to a potentially chaotic entry into the unknown, it also served to connect each and every participant with a shared experience.

Then, at the very first communal event of the actual conference—the orientation—the data about people's intimacy constellations was revealed. It was delivered in a way that made it clear that you are not alone. At its end, everyone would feel they knew with whom they were sharing the tent, and that they had a place in this community. It was a place in which they were connected and where they already knew that they belonged.

---

* For example, locally grown organic fruit and a personal bottle of spring water offered at *chesed*, check in for registration materials at *gevurah*…

Intimacy with Self

*It occurred to me that life is a process of sort of unpeeling
who you are and becoming something, rather than
figuring out what you are supposed to be.*

~ Sarah Slean, singer-songwriter

I AM NOT A MEDITATOR. OKAY, I HAVE ON OCCASION sat quietly, simply watching my thoughts for twenty or thirty minutes, but I have never made a practice of it. My friend Shoshana has, though, and since she spends so much time, mindfully, with herself, I decided to call her and find out what she thought about "Self Intimacy."

I met Shoshana fifteen years ago, when Jack and I first moved out to Colorado. She and her life partner, David, had a home/retreat center up one of the canyon roads outside Boulder. Already for years, both David and Shoshana had had their own meditation practice. For Shoshana, it centered around the Japanese Tea Ceremony. David was, at that point, exploring Jewish meditation. We met when David, at age fifty-five, was in the process of becoming a rabbi. He and Jack had the same teacher.

Our relationship developed in a really fun and full way. Often, especially as we get older, we get to know people slowly, bit by bit. We meet a potential new friend at a meeting, a class, or a party and find that we have some things in common. We invite them for dinner and spend an evening in conversation. They invite us back. Over time, a friendship develops.

Not so with our friendship with David and Shoshana. Our time with them was more like a slumber party. From almost the first moment we met them, our get-togethers were like vacations. We would drive up the canyon, arrive on a Friday afternoon and stay until Sunday. In the span of those forty-eight-hour encounters, wonderful connections and cross connections unfolded. David and Jack related on the rabbinic stuff, and Shoshana and I related as girlfriends … and sisters. David and I related as the more logical/practical, grounded "how's business" member of each couple while Shoshana and Jack were more connected in the air. Together, we'd make dinner, make Shabbos, sing, dance, study Torah, go for walks, drink tea, and just hang out.

The retreat center was custom built by David and Shoshana. It sat on top of a steep hill surrounded by classic Rocky Mountain boulders and pine trees. In addition to their living and office quarters, there were three or four guest rooms, a hermitage retreat tree house, and a tearoom. The guest rooms were all decorated with a very simple Japanese motif: a futon on the floor and rice paper lamps atop a small night table. On retreat, what more do you need?

In addition to facilitating retreats for others, frequently, either David or Shoshana would go "on retreat" themselves, which meant that for forty days, they would withdraw from the outside world in order to be more present with their respective inner world. That meant no talking. No phone calls. No e-mail. No television and no newspapers. No books and no movies. There was a little cooking, a little eating, a little walking. There was a lot of sitting.

When Shoshana yearns to experience something, she has been known to go to extremes. Most recently, she deeply wanted to be able to answer the question "Who am I?" without all the distractions of the outside world. To answer that question, she found that a forty-day retreat was not enough. So, she let go of most of her worldly possessions, withdrew from most of her connections, and moved with David to a small desert town in Western Colorado.

What she found out was that being with oneself is not a whole lot different from being with other people. People who spend a lot of time with themselves (different from simply *by* themselves) end up having a stream of conversations among the different parts of their personalities. If you are engaging in this self-repartee consciously, over many years, you "grow up" the characters inside of you. To accomplish this maturation, you need to go through the same disappointment with pieces of yourself that you go through with people in your life. It is a great place to learn about acceptance.

"We are an organism that responds to life, as life presents itself," Shoshana says. "If the question is 'Who am I?', the next question is 'In what second are you asking?'" When a bird flies overhead, she can be as annoyed at the bird for disturbing her as she can be with people who bother her. That's just one of the characters. Another day, another moment, she could see that same bird and want to take off with it. That's another part of her.

Shoshana says that this process of self-reflection that leads to self-knowledge and self-acceptance has made her more appreciative of others. That is, it enables us to recognize that we all have "multiple personalities" within us. My friend Naomi from the Redwoods, also a meditator, speaks of the personalities as archetypes. We all have within us all the basic literary archetypes. They vary in size and intensity based on the factors that make us unique—where and when we were born, our place in the birth order in our family of origin, our socioeconomic status, our genetics, our life experiences, and a whole slew of other factors that we can only imagine. I sometimes think of the archetypes as my internal board of directors. They often have a meeting to discuss experiences. The better we know our personalities, and archetypes, the deeper our intimacy is with ourselves.

A good level of self-intimacy can keep you out of trouble. Take my phone call with Jack one morning, shortly after our separation. At his regular breakfast phone check-in with David, he asked me if I had a minute. He told me that he had woken up with this dream to make an offer to his current employers about working six months a year. Since he'd been so unhappy there, maybe that would make sense? Would I be willing to talk with him about this? Yes, I said, later...

In the car, on the way back from dropping David at school, my archetypal board of directors began to have a conversation:

The Compassionate One: "Oh, poor Jack. I really feel for him. It must feel like nothing is working out. The Divorce, The Driving, His Health, The Snow, The Job."

The Mother Lion: "What does this mean for David? Is his father going to abandon him? Move away?"

The Fed-Up One: "Why does he have to create such chaos around him? Why can't he just figure it out? Why do I have to be involved?"

The Fearful One: "Oy, is he going to quit working? Then say he can't afford any child support? How will I pay for summer camp, eyeglasses, new shoes, the mortgage?"

The Wise One: "Wow, I am more than a little triggered by this. I want to be supportive and I can see he is open to support, but I don't think it is such a good idea to have this conversation without some rules or a well-defined agenda."

The Honest One: "I'm going to call him and tell him what I've been thinking …."

The Cautious One: "… that today I do not have time to give this quality time, and suggest …"

The Problem Solver: "… that next Wednesday he and I and Daniel get together for an hour to specifically talk with him about what he really wants, and what he really needs, and realistically what his options are."

All in favor? None opposed. Motion passed. Meeting adjourned.

Faith in the Journey of the Soul

*My religion consists of a humble admiration
of the illimitable superior spirit who reveals himself
in the slight details we are able to perceive
with our frail and feeble mind.*

~ Albert Einstein, theoretical physicist

IT IS HARD TO IMAGINE THE SUFFERING OF A mother who gives birth to a terminally ill baby. In the human world of emotions, it is tragic. Nine months of hopes and dreams, anticipation and planning, all evaporating in a moment of realization that there is no future. In the spiritual world, however, I have faith that the angels know what they are doing. What seems like an incomplete life to us is likely a completed journey for the soul.

Linnea was five months old and had SMA: spinal muscular atrophy. I found out about Linnea from a colleague of Jack's, who is a chaplain in the Army as well as a congregational rabbi nearby who had been contacted by Linnea's grandfather (who was also a chaplain in the Army). An e-mail arrived asking if there was anyone nearby who might be able to take care of this couple's healthy two-year-old or sit in the hospital with Linnea in order to give the parents a break. I went to the hospital every Friday morning for weeks.

I am told SMA is basically infantile Lou Gehrig's disease. It is a genetic aberration where not enough protein is made to signal the muscles to move. What that means is that Linnea had no muscle development or control. She could not move herself around at all. When I arrived, the nurse came into the room to help me get Linnea situated from the bed into my lap. We used pillows on my right arm to prop up her head and to make sure that all the tubes (oxygen mostly) weren't tangled. She was only five months old, so she couldn't speak to tell me if something was uncomfortable. She couldn't even adjust her own legs. She couldn't put her fingers in her mouth to suck, nor could she swallow. Last week, they took the feeding tube from her nose and put it directly into her stomach. Eventually, she will stop breathing and then she will die. There is no cure.

On the human plane, it feels tragic. A baby is going to die. But ...

... from a spiritual, Everything-Is-One perspective, who are we to say anything about the journey of the soul? Linnea was here for just a short visit. In that short span of time, her life had already, deeply, impacted mine.

The One Who Knows
Me Intimately

Now, if someone says to me, 'I'm not spiritual,' I'll say,
'You breathe, don't you?' Well, that's spiritual.
Spirituality is breath, and you take it from there.

~ Vernon Harper, Northern Cree, Canada

A FEW YEARS AGO, I HAD A TWO-MINUTE experience that opened up the world of Spiritual Intimacy. Although there was a time in my life when I was drawn to understand Jewish religious practice as part of my birthright, and while I have incorporated profound parts of home-based Jewish practice into my life, I have never been ignited by mainstream Jewish religious practice. Using the prayer book, especially, has always been an alienating experience. I've often said that going to services distracts me from my spiritual life. I simply felt that the theology in the book did not at all mirror or articulate my experience of the spiritual.

Spirituality, for me, is about the interconnectedness of everything, a sense of being a part of the cosmic web of energy. Like Deepak Chopra talking about God as "energy and information" and like Rabbi David A. Cooper talking about "God is a Verb." I just didn't get it from the prayer book.

Having said that, the two-minute experience that opened up the spiritual world of prayer for me was a lesson I learned from a rabbi while studying the prayer book. The class was called "The *Siddur* (prayer book) as a Spiritual Path." It was taught by Rabbi Marcia Prager.

I had heard amazing things about Reb Marcia as a teacher, and while I knew her personally, I had never studied with her. I was, at that time, on a leisurely six-week vacation in Philadelphia, visiting friends and family, nostalgically studying Tai Chi with my old teacher, and walking every day in the Wissahickon, watching the daily changes of autumn. It just so happened that Reb Marcia was offering a six-week class and in I jumped, studying the prayer book every Thursday morning with her and a dozen other students in her living room. In some way, it was my last chance to look at the disconnected God language of the prayer book and see if I could find a place where I would feel at home.

I enjoyed the class. I knew a few people there, and it was nice to see them and learn with them. The information presented was interesting. Hmm, you might be thinking, "enjoyed," "nice," "interesting"—it doesn't sound like the makings of a profound experience. The truth is that the first few classes were just that: enjoyable, nice, and interesting. The day of my profound experience started in the same way: enjoyable, nice, and interesting. As the class was nearing its end, I asked a question.

Most of you probably aren't that familiar with Jewish liturgy, so I'll take a brief moment to tell you something. There is a name for God that is used all the time. It is made up of four Hebrew letters.* It is the basis for the words Jehovah and Yaweh. We are not really completely sure about the word, but we are taught that we no longer know how it is pronounced. It is some form of the verb "to be" that incorporates past, present, and future and it is said to be an abbreviation for a much longer word that has been lost. Legend has it that the High Priest in days of old (before there were rabbis) would call out this name for God in the inner sanctuary of the Temple in Jerusalem on Yom Kippur. This priest would have a rope tied around his body so in case the experience left him unable to walk out on his own, he could be pulled out.

So, we don't even try to pronounce the word. Instead, when we see those four letters, we say "*Adonai,*" which usually translates as "My Lord." So even though the four letters appear frequently— like all the time in our most common prayers—we don't say them.

---

* It is called the Tetragrammaton and is made up of the letters *yud, hey, vav,* and *hey,* approximately Y-H-V-H in English.

We have our basic prayer pattern "*Baruch Ata* (four letters but instead we say) *Adonai*," "Blessed are you, My Lord." This is the first phrase of all the common prayers… we use it all the time—while lighting the *Hanukah* and *Shabbat* candles, blessing bread and wine, etc.

I had a number of issues with this God-is-Lord language.

There's the cultural piece—America was founded in opposition to the feudal system of Lord and servant. Here in America, no one's gonna lord it over us. Furthermore, as a woman raised with feminist consciousness, that is not the kind of relationship I want with any plant, man, animal, or God. As I studied the prayer book, I saw how often we were replacing the verbalization of the cosmic tetragrammaton of Being into a Lord. No wonder I couldn't relate.

So at ten minutes before the end of class, I asked Reb Marcia, "When did we start replacing YHVH with *Adonai* and isn't there some other term that wouldn't be so alienating that we can use instead?" Reb Marcia folded her hands in her lap and sighed deeply. It wasn't the first time she had before her a student who was wrestling with barriers such as these and it wouldn't be the last. Let's face it, there's plenty of text that slaps our twenty-first-century sensibilities in the face. But Reb Marcia comes from a school where they are not so fast to throw things away. Instead, they look deeper, turning the struggle to the light at every angle to see what gems might be found.

Reb Marcia started talking about the word *Adonai*. She taught us that kabbalistically, each of the ten circles of cosmic energy have one or more assigned names of God and that *Adonai* is in "*Malkhut*"—the circle of royalty and completion. It lies in the center column of "knowing," with the column of "force" at its right and "form" on its left. It shares its space with "*Shekhinah*," the feminine, indwelling name of God. She taught us that the root of the word is *Adon*, which is usually translated as "Lord" but can also be translated as "Master". She invited us to think of Master not as Lord in the sense of a master—servant relationship, but Master in the sense of one who has mastered something. "What does it mean to master something?" she asked.

I had some thoughts and ideas about that. To be a master of something means to have integrated it wholly into your being. It is an intimate knowledge that dissolves all boundaries between the doing of the action and the being of the soul. Isaac Stern (may his memory be for a blessing) was a master violin player. He and the violin were one being and the music that emanated from his togetherness with that instrument was magical. Tiger Woods is master golfer. The club is an extension of his arms and the arc of the ball seems to be directed by his soul. Bobby Fisher is a chess master. He becomes one with the game. That thing with me and maps—some might call me a master wayfinder.

Most of us have had the experience of feeling that something is "second nature." I watch my son David, now ten, tie his shoes. It used to take intense concentration. Now it is second nature. When I was a young teenager, I played guitar—mostly folk songs. Now at forty-nine, I can pick up a guitar and although I am not sure I know the chords for a certain song, my fingers take me there. These "second nature" experiences are a peek into the world of spiritual intimacy—that place of deep connection and union with the cosmic web.

What Reb Marcia said next was followed by awed silence and took me years to integrate into my spiritual practice. She suggested that rather than translate *Adonai* as "My Lord," we should try a different translation: "That Which Knows Me Intimately."

That suggestion changed everything.

Intimate Legacies

There is no end. There is no beginning.
There is only the infinite passion of life.

~ Federico Fellini, film maker

I'VE BEEN PRACTICING MANAGEMENT CONSULTING in one form or another for thirty-eight years. Since that day in the sixth grade when the principal, Miss Rockefeller, asked if I would cover the front office for a few hours because both she and her secretary, Mrs. Verona, would be out of the building,* one of my specialties has been "Eleventh Hour" rescue management. When organizations find themselves hanging on the edge of a cliff and they are unsure whether they want to fly, jump, climb, retreat, or just hang on, they have relied upon me to bring a calm and clear-headed presence to the scene. More than once, I've had the title "Interim Executive Director," because someone either quit or just wasn't up to the task. One such case occurred a few years ago, when I was asked to come in as Interim Executive Director for the Reb Zalman Legacy Project.†

In the Jewish tradition, it is incumbent upon us to honor our teachers. Rabbi Zalman Schachter-Shalomi, better known as "Reb Zalman," was born in Poland in 1924 and fled the Nazi oppression in 1938, finally landing in New York City in 1941. He was

---

* This was 1969. She came into the library and asked me to come into the hallway. I was chewing gum and I thought she was going to reprimand me for that. Instead she asked me to pick a friend and bring my lunch the next day. My best friend, Suzanne Tremblay and I spent the whole afternoon in the principal's office, answering the phones, etc. I remember a 2nd grader came in and had pooped in his pants. We had to deal with that. Can you imagine a principal doing that today? Ah! those innocent times.

† Visit http://www.rzlp.org/

ordained by the Lubavitcher Hasidim in 1947, and in the 1960s, with his fellow revolutionary Rabbi Shlomo Carlebach (1925-1994), he traveled to the West Coast. There, he "brought about a renewal of Jewish life by speaking in the cultural vernacular"* and earned the title "Hippie Rabbi." Today, it's more like "Cyber Rebbe," as he gracefully weaves images from the world of technology with his universal spiritual lessons.

In his lifetime, Reb Zalman went beyond the Jewish path to experience God. He engaged in ecumenical dialogue with leaders of many spiritual paths, from Trappist monks to Sufi sheikhs. Although he has described himself as a "spiritual peeping-Tom," he actually has deep learning in the theory and practice of many traditions. Over time, he developed intimate friendships with many of the world's great spiritual teachers, including Father Thomas Merton, Reverend Howard Thurman, Pir Vilayat Inayat-Khan, Ken Wilber, and the fourteenth Dalai Lama.

In the mid 1990s, Reb Zalman was named the World Wisdom Chair at Naropa University, the only accredited Buddhist-inspired university in the Western hemisphere. He was the first non-Buddhist to be so honored. It is there that The Reb Zalman Legacy Project was established to preserve, develop, and disseminate his teachings. Given all the planning and attention that was going into the Legacy Project, it seemed only natural for me to speak to Reb Zalman about the Intimacy of Legacy.

We sat together in his meditation/prayer room in his home in Boulder that often doubles as an intimate meeting space. The walls are filled with the evidence of just how far and wide Reb Zalman has traveled—spiritually—in his lifetime. Books on ecumenism (inter-religious dialogue), contemplative practice, ecology, gerontology, and psychology of religion, are next to those of Jewish law and mysticism. He has ritual objects from a range of traditions that serve to inspire prayer and devotion.

On my agenda was the future. I wanted to hear from this teacher of thousands what it meant to be leaving a legacy and what

* Visit http://www.rzlp.org/

he thought about the idea of transmitting intimacy beyond one's lifetime. I had expected the conversation to jump into the future—Zalman was often jumping into the future. "Imagine," he once said, "that if they were to rebuild the Temple (multi-faith) and that as you enter, your brain gets scanned, and based on the images that work for you, a holographic image of your prayer space appears." He was always ahead of his time and I imagined my conversation with him would include sparks of the future.

Instead, this great rabbi of our modern times went humbly to the past. Reb Zalman spoke to me of the relationship he had with his teachers of the past—with his Rebbe*, and even back to the founder of Hasidic Judaism: the Baal Shem Tov†. He spoke about how the gravesites of these Rebbes hold a power for him, that when visiting those graves he can feel the link through time, the connection beyond culture. A few months prior, he had gone to the Ukraine to visit the gravesite of the Baal Shem Tov. He recalled how he had made a powerful, intimate connection with this great Rebbe at that moment. He felt that the Baal Shem had spoken to him, saying, "God is always sending down good stuff, but some people build dams and control the outlet, making the hole where the good stuff can flow smaller and smaller. I came and dug under the dam to make a bigger hole so it should flow again. It is how you have also done and why I count you as part of my legacy."

I'd like to think that in my small way, I too am an extension of that legacy—digging under the dam—chipping away at that narrow hole that says that monogamy, marriage, and procreation are the goals and the best way for everyone to make a family, thereby increasing the flow of good connections in every direction.

Thank you, Zalman, for hosting the party and passing out the chisels.

---

* Yosef Yitzchok Schneersohn (the sixth Lubavitcher rebbe, 1880—1950)
† (1698—1760)

Knowing From Where We Came

If you forget who you are, you cannot live in peace.
That's why I enjoy showing people that
my culture is alive and well.

~ Omar Suazo, Garifuna, Central America

WITH THE BREAKDOWN OF INTERGENERA-
tional living and the mobility of our society, we
are suffering from a deficiency of Transgenerational
Intimacy. The days of tribal living are long gone, and that of three
generations living in the same town (let alone the same house) is
a fading memory. There are no longer elders in our lives to tell us
the stories of our ancestors and our history. There are no longer so
many aunts, uncles, and cousins around us to witness as we make
mistakes, learn, have successes, and become full-fledged members
of the family and community.

It used to be that neighborhoods were intimate communities. For better or worse, the vast number of people in our daily
lives knew about our joys and sorrows. When we were sick,
someone would be there to help with the children, and a pot of
soup would appear on the doorstep. Robert Putnam, in *Bowling
Alone*, paints a clear picture of how, for our culture as a whole,
our social connections have collapsed. There is a void and we try
to fill the void with things: toys, bigger houses, cars, and high-
tech equipment. We get our stories from television and gossip
magazines, but they are not *our* stories and somehow that just
doesn't feed our soul.

It is a basic and natural course of human development for
older people to tell their stories to young people. Dodi tells me
that in her Sunflower Center, where she spends the day with six

toddlers, the oral tradition is strong. The children themselves have shared experiences and they want her to tell the stories over and over—about how they planted seeds and things grew, about how Maury hurt his head, and about how Molly got older and went off to preschool.

I never met either of my grandfathers. My paternal grandfather died when my father was twenty-one, while undergoing routine prostate surgery. His blood pressure shot up during the operation and he died. My maternal grandfather died when my mom was three. I have vague memories of my paternal grandmother, Nanny. I remember her lullabies and I remember she taught me my first card game (Donkey—a version of hands-down). She died when I was ten and had suffered a mild stroke a few years before. I heard stories of what a great cook she was, especially her baking. I have what is left of her dishes—eight dinner plates, three dessert plates, and a serving platter. I also have some pictures.

Oddly enough, the grandparent whose stories I feel most connected with is my maternal grandmother. I hardly remember my Bubbie. She died when I was in first grade. I remember her as an old lady, frail and shriveled, with a smile on her face and a blanket covering her legs. She never learned to speak English (except the phrase "I love you"), and in the end, she suffered with dementia. But by listening to her children, her life story has come alive.

Bubbie was born in 1887 in a *shtetl* in Russia. Life was simple and resources were meager. Clothes were washed in the river and bread was baked daily to feed the family. As a young woman, Bubbie married Isaac and one, two, three, she had four children. When the youngest wasn't yet walking, Isaac left for Philadelphia with plans to send for the family. Within a year, he sent tickets for the boat. Bubbie and her four little ones traveled two days, only to be turned away. My Uncle Ben had a contagious eye infection and they wouldn't let him on the boat. Resigned to their fate, they went home, planning to make the trip again when the infection had cleared. World War I and the Russian Revolution spoiled that plan. It would be ten years until Bubbie and Isaac would reunite.

During that time, Bubbie became a peddler and went around all the neighboring towns selling cotton, needles, and thread. Mostly it was barter—a bit of this for a bit of that. She also sold tobacco. The problem was that after the Russian Revolution, the selling of tobacco became contraband—illegal. You could be shot for selling it. But for Bubbie it made the difference between getting what she needed to provide for her growing family of five and not, so she kept selling it. One day, she found herself in a neighboring town where there was a *pogrom** and her life was in danger. But luck and good fortune were on her side, and a sympathetic peasant family let her hide in their basement. She was there for two weeks, with her children at home not knowing where she was.

There are stories of other hardships, like the fire that burned their house to the ground, and the time Uncle Jack fell through the ice into a lake (they thought was frozen) when they were returning from peddling. Bubbie endured, and her children thrived.

Finally, in 1923, they again made the 2-day trip by horse and cart. Isaac had sent them 2nd class tickets but somewhere along the line, some unknown, uncaring administrator sold them and now they had tickets for Steerage. When Bubbie complained, the administrator asked, "Do you want to go to America?" Steerage it was.

Finally, after ten years of separation, Bubbie and Isaac were reunited. Three years later, my mother was born. Three years after that, while getting off a trolley on a rainy, windy day, Isaac was tragically hit by a motorcycle and died. That was 1929 and the year of the crash and the beginning of the Great Depression. Bubbie once again became a single mother and the bread-winner for her family. She took over the butcher shop business Isaac had built and was a determined businesswoman. As my mother tells it, Bubbie

---

* Organized and often officially sanctioned attacks or massacres of Jews living in small Jewish communities in Russia.

never let a customer leave the store without buying something.*

Bubbie's eldest, my Aunt Clara, got married and the three brothers got older, and at some point, Bubbie had an offer of marriage from a decent gentleman. Evidently not decent enough, though. She would have to stop working and could only bring her youngest, my mother, with her if she married him. The boys would be on their own. She said no.

She spent the next thirty years as a kosher butcher. In the end, with the beginning of dementia apparent and unable to care for herself, her children moved her into a very fancy nursing home. In quiet protest, she stopped eating. So they all chipped in every month and got her an apartment and a live-in companion.

Bubbie lived several more years there, in her own home. That is when I knew her: old and crinkled and smelling of mothballs. Looking at her then, who would have known the hardships she overcame and the strength and grace with which she overcame them. I didn't know any of those stories then, but knowing them now, I can see that strength and determination in my mother and I like to think that I can see them in myself. Bubbie died on March 17, 1965.† Although I barely knew her, through her story I feel an intimate connection with her. May her memory be for a blessing.

---

* My mother also recalls that while some of her classmates were suffering with the Depression—for example, having to share one cupcake between two sisters—my mother would get a little hungry and go into the butcher shop and grab herself a couple of lamb chops for dinner.

† In the Jewish calendar, it was the 13th day of the month of Adar—the Fast of Esther.

Transmitting into the Future

With storytelling we enter the trance of the sacred.
Telling stories reminds us of our humanity
in this beautiful broken world.

~ Terry Tempest Williams, author, naturalist
and environmental activist

WHEN MY SON WAS BORN, ONE OF THE gifts he got was a "Time Capsule" kit. My childhood friend, Terri, gave it to him. She was always the picture taker and the documenter of events, so this was a natural and authentic gift from her. The kit consisted of a big tin container, a booklet with pages to fill out, and suggestions for what to put in the tin. In the booklet were questions such as how much things cost the year of the birth and how much we think they will cost when we open the time capsule. My parents and sisters and nieces wrote letters and so did my son's sister and some of our beloved friends. On David's twenty-fifth birthday, we'll invite everyone who wrote letters (those still alive) to come party with us.

I threw lots of sentimental things in there: the outfit David was wearing at his *bris* and one of those teeny-weeny diapers newborns wear. Another thing I put in the capsule was my two favorite episodes of *Star Trek the Next Generation*: "The Probe" and "Darmok."

"The Probe" (technically titled "Inner Light") is an especially poignant example of Character Intimacy because the story itself is about such intimacy. If it's been a while since you've seen it, or if you've never had the pleasure, I'll give you the CliffsNote version.

The Starship Enterprise encounters an apparently unmanned probe. (It is apparently "unwomanned" as well.) Suddenly, a low-level nucleonic particle stream is projected from the probe and tethers itself to the brain waves of Captain Picard. He falls to the floor. For the next forty minutes, we occasionally get glimpses into the urgency and distress of Picard's crew on the Enterprise, but mostly we are sharing the experience that Picard, himself, is having in his mind.

He has found himself on the planet Kataan, in what feels like it could be a parallel life. In this parallel life, his name is Kamin and he has a wife, Aileen (Picard never married is his Starship life), and a best friend, Batai. Apparently, he lives a quiet existence as an iron weaver (although he is told he prefers to play the flute) in a simple civilized community called Ressick.

He is at first very disoriented—his wife tells him he's had a fever for days—and he desperately wants to get back to his ship. We feel with him his confusion and then anger and frustration as he tries to make sense of what is happening.

We witness a ritual in the community: the planting of a sapling that will be kept alive despite the drought that the planet is experiencing—a foreshadowing of the future of the planet.

The time passes in his new life, and we witness Picard's gradual acceptance that this is his life as Kamin. We feel his growing love and respect for his wife and we experience the joy and pride he feels at the birth of his two children—whom we see as little ones and then as young adults. We have glimpses into the sweet, gentle nature of the people on Kataan—how they greet each other and say "Go Carefully" as they part. Back to real time on the Starship Enterprise, the crew is quite distressed. Their attempt to disrupt the particle beam causes all of Picard's systems and vital signs go into chaos. They re-establish the beam.

Back to Kataan, years pass for Kamin and we feel the experience with him. He plays his flute as a way to spend some quiet time with himself. We understand that he has developed a deep intimacy with his daughter, whom he has trained as a scientist and who works by his side studying the effects of the now disastrous drought on the soil. Kamin struggles with the choices his grown son is making as he chooses music over science.

As foreshadowed, the drought on Kataan has worsened, and we

learn that the planet is dying. On the Enterprise, they have learned that this probe came from one of six planets in a star system, in which the sun went nova and all life ceased 1,000 years prior. As Kamin ages, he has also come to realize the impending fate of the planet. He has accumulated data from soil studies, which he presents to the official, showing that the planet is dying. The official confides that the government scientists came to the same conclusion two years prior. They speak about how—because they are only beginning to explore space technology in the most rudimentary way—they don't have many options for saving even a small portion of the population. Kamin, now so deeply caring about his home, implores the official, "You simply cannot let this civilization die!" That conversation is interrupted by Kamin's son, pulling him home. There we witness a deeply moving scene: Kamin with his wife in the final moments of her life. Simply from Patrick Stewart's subtle body and facial expressions (he's such a good actor), we know how deeply he has come to love her.

The final scene on Kataan takes place years later. Kamin is very old and is playing with his grandson on the floor, as his daughter invites him outside to watch the launching of the probe. "What probe?" he says. "No one told me about any probe." For a moment, Time and Space seem to stand still. Kamin's daughter says, "You knew about it, Father. You've already seen it." A young image of his long-ago-deceased old friend Batai appears and says, "We hoped our probe would encounter someone in the future, someone who could be a teacher, someone who could tell others about us."

Kamin/Picard, trembling and beginning to sob, says, "It's *me*, *I'm* the someone. It is the launching of the probe that finds *me* in the future!"

His wife, Aileen then appears, looking as she did when we first met her forty years earlier. Kamin/Picard is moved beyond words to see her again. He mouths her name "Aileen" and she says, "The rest of us have been gone 1,000 years. If you remember what we were then and how we lived, we will have found life again. Now we live in you. Tell them of us, my darling."

Cut to the Enterprise. The particle stream has stopped as suddenly as it began. Picard comes to and immediately asks Riker how long he was out. Riker says "About twenty or twenty-five minutes." We, along with Picard, are in disbelief. How could that have been only twenty-five minutes? It was a whole intimate lifetime of experience!

The probe is examined and it is found that all systems have shut down. The only thing on board is a flute. The final scene of the show is Captain Picard in his quarters, playing a simple melody that he had composed during his life on Kataan.* We know that Picard intimately knows the people of Kataan—who they were and how they lived. The probe succeeded in its mission.†

---

* The episode is named after the piece "Inner Light" by Jay Chattaway.

† USA Today reports that the brass Ressikan flute was one of the items up for bid at the Christie's official studio auction of Star Trek memorabilia, which took place on October 5-7, 2006. The flute, which cannot actually be played, was originally estimated to have a sale price of $300. Auction directors admitted that their estimates for many items did not "factor in that emotional fury generated around this kind of material." The estimate was later raised to $800-$1,200 on Christie's website.

In the days leading up to the auction, Denise Okuda, former Trek scenic artist and video supervisor as well as co-writer of the auction catalog, stated that "That's the item people say they really have to have, because it's so iconic to a much-beloved episode." The final bid for the flute at the auction was $40,000. Including the additional twenty-percent fee Christie's collected on all items from the winning bidder, the total price for the flute was $48,000.

An Ethical Will

Don't ask yourself what the worlds needs,
ask yourself what makes you come alive.
And then go and do that.
Because what the world needs
is people who have come alive.

~ Howard Thurman, author, philosopher, theologian,
educator and civil rights leader

THE STAR TREK STORY, AS COMPELLING AS IT IS, IS fiction. While we can't compress the essence of our existence into a transformational twenty-minute brain-zapping experience, we do have some viable options. The Ethical Will is a good start.

I am an older mom. I was thirty-nine when I gave birth. When David is fifty, I will—God willing—be 89. I hope to know his children as my parents have known him. I can't even hope to know my great-grandchildren, but I can leave a trail so that they can know me. For them, I have started a family photo album. I have photos that go back as far back as photos existed. I have also thought deeply about who I am, and about the part of me that can transcend time.

I believe that intimacy can be conveyed beyond a lifetime—as a source of comfort and inspiration for the generations to come. While I have been motivated to write an Ethical Will for my son, it is really for me. While I'm alive, it serves as guidance for my life-practice. Through the values clarification that naturally occurs in this process, I deepen my knowledge of self. The writing of an Ethical Will can stimulate a myriad of unexpected intimate connections. If I choose to write my Ethical Will as part of a group—for example, as an extension of a study group or other circle of companions—the witnessing will intensify the bonds among group members. When I discuss my Ethical Will with friends and family, it can serve to strengthen those already intimate relationships. After I've finished the human journey, it is intended for anyone who will want to know, more deeply, who I was.

I have eighteen points in my ethical will that I continue to expand and refine. As an example, below I have included four of those points. In addition to deeper thoughts on the eighteen points, I'm planning to add sections on My Favorites (books, movies, friends, heroes, vacations, etc. and why they are my favorites). At some point, I'll make a video recording, too, because as powerful as words are, nothing beats the visual, non-verbal human in action.

What follows is, by definition, a work in progress as I continue to reflect on what is important, valuable and life-affirming for me. I say a work-in-progress for two reasons: That as I peel away at the layers to uncover the essence of my own truths, I continue to refine this list; and that I, myself, am a work- in-progress—that while I aim to live guided by these principles, there are plenty of moments when the practice lags and the arrow is off the mark. Please don't read my list as things you should be doing. You have your own values that come from your own unique nature/nurture experience of this lifetime.*

Four of the Eighteen Reminders Which Help Sustain the Quality of My Life

1) Move Your Body Every Day
I know this practice will help to keep all my systems healthy. If I have some physical limitations, I don't let that stop me — I just keep moving within the constraints of my limitations. The movement doesn't need to be aerobic and it I don't need to spend money to join a gym (although neither of those are bad things). Stretching,

---

* If you want to do this for yourself, there are lots of resources available. What I used as a starting point was a simple paradigm of the four worlds—physical, emotional, intellectual and spiritual—and began reflecting on lessons I've learned in each of these "worlds."

lifting, walking, parking further from the entrance, a little yoga…
these are all good ways to move my body. I learned this from
watching my parents. I notice that flexibility and strength spill into
all parts of my life.

2) Recovery From Conflict is a Golden Opportunity

Ninety-five percent of the time,* someone's negative reaction to
me is not really about me. It is filtered through their lifetime of
experiences—traumas, wounds and disappointments—from their
lives. I don't take it personally. At the same time, I take my own
stuff very personally, because similarly, when I am triggered by
someone, it is likely that it is more about me than about them. Carl
Jung (1875—1961) said, "Everything that irritates us about others
can lead us to an understanding of ourselves." I work hard to reveal
myself to myself, to acknowledge my shadow and to illuminate my
blind spots. I prioritize this as important ongoing personal work.

Conflict happens, and given the idea above, we often don't
know where it really started. The recovery from that conflict is
a most powerful healing salve. When I notice that someone has
recoiled defensively at something I said, I aim to quickly recover
(within 24-hours) with a small apology, such as "I noticed some
tension between us. If what I said offended you, please accept my
apology. No offense was intended."

The more intimate the relationship, the more hurtful it can feel
and the more healing the apology can be. For the deeper conflicts
with the most intimate of relationships, I remind myself not to be
afraid to say, "I know you so well that I know how deeply what
I did/said hurt you. I am sorry I went to that wounded place of
yours. Please forgive me."

3) There's Always Another Way

When I find myself at an impasse, I know that I can always find
a way out. I may decide to build a ladder to climb over it, borrow

---

* I made up that number. There is no way to actually measure it, but anecdotally,
  I know you'll agree that the percentage is high.

a pole to vault over it, blast a hole and go through it, or go backwards to find another route altogether. For inspiration, I look to designs in nature for new ideas or I pick up a book or magazine on an unfamiliar topic. Sometimes I take a walk or a shower or I call a friend or colleague for advice. Often I simply sit and contemplate, letting the time pass to a new moment. I know that whatever road block I encounter, that there is always another way to deal with it. On of my favorite quotes is by John W. Gardner. He said, "Creativity requires the freedom to consider 'unthinkable' alternatives, to doubt the worth of cherished practices."

If I want something to happen, I have to make it happen. When I hear myself complaining, I stop and assess if a) the complaint is directed at someone who can do something about it and b) if I can offer constructive input toward a resolution. If neither a nor b applies, I do my best to stop, because I know that complaining erects a barrier between me and my seeing another way.

That's not to say that finding another way is always easy. Change is difficult. Habits are hard to break and sometimes change means swimming against the current. Early in my personal and professional life, I learned a key ingredient in the change process, that "If you can't measure it, you can't manage it" (Peter Drucker). But that's just part of the process. Awareness, strategy selection, and action are also important. That's the equation for change. And, there is one more critical piece that sometimes gets lost in our fast-paced, instant-gratification world: Reflection. As times moves on, and I and the people around me grow, I strive to reflect on whether the old strategy is still the best strategy. I have to remember to allow enough time and space for reflection.

4) Don't Assume You Know Anything Except That Everything Is One.

Everything is connected. All that I do, say, think, and feel has a rippling effect on the world around me. When I smile at someone, I have an impact on them and on the next person they interact with. If I leave my shoes in the middle of the stairway, someone else's path will be blocked, and that irritation may spill into their next interaction. When I trust someone, they become more effective in the world. Similarly, I am effected by the actions, thoughts, feelings, and beings of others.

Assumptions weaken connections. Whenever I assume something about the "other" without really knowing them—for example, how happy they are, what their interests might be, and what they believe about things that are important to me—I compromise the integrity of the web of cosmic connection. I love it when someone "blows" my stereotype—the woman who appears lacking (no marriage, no children, not much money) who is deeply engaged with life, the grandma into video games, the enlisted military officer with progressive politics. I remind myself how disconnected I've felt when people assumed things about me because of, for example, who I was married to and then I inquire rather than assume.

The lines of connection are already there among all that I encounter: Animals, the food I eat, the information I gather, and especially among people. Tending to these connections is a good thing and brings me more strongly, intimately, in relationship with the Source of All.

Unexpected Intimacy Revealed

Strategies for Evolving Intimate Connections

Vitality arises from sheer human contact, especially from loving connections. This makes the people we care about most an elixir of sorts, an ever-renewing source of energy. The neural exchange between a grandparent and a toddler, between lovers or a satisfied couple, or among good friends has palpable virtues ... the practical lesson for us all comes down to... Nourish your social connections.

~ Daniel Goleman, author of *Social Intelligence: The New Science of Human Relationships*

It's E.A.S.Y

Tell me and I forget.
Teach me and I remember.
Involve me and I learn.

~ Benjamin Franklin, author, political theorist, politician,
printer, scientist, inventor, civic activist, and diplomat

T HIS CHAPTER IS THE "HOW TO" PORTION OF
Unexpected Intimacy. I have a little fear whenever I start a
How To. That's because I've been told by many readers that
what they love best about my writing is my intimate conversational
style. When I go into How To mode, I'm afraid I'll lose that intimacy and just sound preachy.

With that caveat revealed up front, I'm going to talk about one
way to approach evolving your own constellation of intimate connections. I think easy works best, so I'm gonna make it easy—four
steps that are E.A.S.Y: E(xpectations), A(ction), S(ocial lubrication), Y(ou in the universe).

In the work that follows, I assume you have read the stories in
Unexpected Intimacy, Everyday Connections that Nourish the Soul.
If you haven't, go ahead and read the prologue and a few selected
stories. This familiarization will ensure that you have expanded
and refined your own definition of "intimacy."

Two parts from the prologue bear repeating: why I wrote this
book and a working definition of intimacy.

Why did I write the book? In our busy, fast-forward 21ˢᵗ century lives, one of the first things to suffer is our relationships. On
top of that, the newest research shows that health and happiness
are inextricably tied to the quality of our social connections. We
need both a fresh perspective on relationships and a straightforward way to strengthen our connections. *Unexpected Intimacy*
provides both.

What is the definition of intimacy? Intimacy is deep knowing. One can have intimacy with a subject, an experience, a place, oneself, and of course, other people. Although the stories in *Unexpected Intimacy* cover all those topics and more, in this "how to" we deal with people. Any time you really see, hear, understand, or witness the experience of another, you are part of an intimate moment. Any time your experience is witnessed by another, you are part of an intimate moment. Moments don't make relationships, but when there is a consistency in the exchange of intimate moments in a relationship, that relationship can be considered intimate.

In the material that follows, we will consider both intimate moments and intimate relationships. Moments can be seen as seeds for intimate relationships, and both forms of intimacy are nourishing to the soul.

BEFORE WE BEGIN... CHOICE AND CHANGE: These are the biggest challenges in the 21st century. Did you know that there are 17,000 new "food products" introduced in America every year, with $32 billion spent by the food industry to let us know about them? Did you know that if you search on the keyword "relationships" in books at Amazon.com, you will be presented with 561,856 choices and six different ways to sort them? Did you know that if you Google "yoga mat," you will be faced with 1,580,000 possibilities?

Never before in the history of the human race has choice looked like this. When we were hunters, our choices were raw, rare, or well done. When we became farmers, our choices were more complex: where to put the fields, how much land to till, and which plants to grow. Today, the number of choices we make in one stop at the grocery store alone would be enough to send our ancestors into shock.

On the one hand, we are like kids in a candy store, consuming information like it was nectar from the Gods. On the other hand, the amount of data coming at us is at least distracting and confusing us. It may even be making us sick. One of the things we need to learn, as a species, is that the quality of the outcome is not always increased by the quantity of the input.

Obviously, some of our choices are weightier than others, and that tendency may influence how much data we need to collect. But unless we stay conscious of whether or not we need more information, the world is going to overwhelm us with it. Metaphors can be helpful here... We may need to cover our ears, carry a shield, close the door or build a wall because when we reach the point of overwhelm, it doesn't really matter if we are choosing ice cream or buying a house. We are equally paralyzed.

> *...one choice, to make one change*
> *is all you need to begin...*

Change is a whole other can of worms. Fortunately, decades of research give us hope and a template for success. Information on change is presented at the end of this section, on pages 228-231.

In the meantime, one thing we know for sure is that you don't need to overwhelm yourself—one choice, to make one change is all you need to begin shifting the energy you have for connecting.

Tips for Managing Choice
- Listen to your gut before reviewing "the facts."
- Shield yourself from excessive input.
- Let in only what you want in.
- Get off lists that don't engage you.
- Limit TV. Mute commercials.
- Don't be seduced by FMS (Fear of Missing Something).
- Ask, "Do I really need more information?"
- "Is what I have now, enough?"
- Take care not to take on too much
- Make sure your choice lifts your energy rather than depletes it.

E(xpectations)

*It is only when we cannot change the experience that we
look for ways to change our view of the experience.*

~ Daniel Gilbert, author, *Stumbling on Happiness*

The best-kept secret is that how we view our expectations about our relationships is the key to happy and healthy connections. If you catch yourself feeling disappointed in current relationships or hear yourself saying, "I don't have anyone in my life with whom I can share ..." then you are a candidate for some work in the area of expectations.

I know this tendency first hand because nothing upsets me more than disappointment and disappointment is what happens when I am not monitoring my expectations. The best way to describe it is like the "Rocket Crash" that can happen when I meet someone new and get so excited—high even—thinking about how this person has all the qualities my Intimacy Constellation is lacking and that s/he will become a deep, lifelong friend. It is only when we take our first long walk together that s/he reveals her/himself to be nothing like the person I thought s/he was. Only then do I ask myself, "What was I thinking?"

On the other hand, take the "Hidden Treasure" relationship – the person I find crossing my path in different settings. On our first encounter, we may start out with a nod across the room to acknowledge we are both present, or we may exchange a few words. The next few times our paths cross, we make a little pleasant small talk. In the process, we get to know a little about each other and realize that we have some points of connection. That commonality starts to happen more frequently, and eventually—maybe weeks, maybe months, or maybe even years later—one of us takes the bold step and makes an invitation. With each new shared experience, our connection takes a small step up. As it continues its ascent, we one day realize that we've become important and nourishing parts of each other's lives.

Take my relationship with Ty. Last year, I met Ty at an evening lecture on self-publishing. He was sitting next to me. At that point, I was well advanced in the publishing process and was offering some suggestions to those who were just beginning. At the end of class, Ty asked me for my business card. He followed up with me a few months later with some questions. Then, grateful for my help, he reached out again, this time with information for me about a book event. Since I felt we had already developed a flow of give and take, the next time Ty contacted me, I made a proposal that we be author/book promotion co-coaching buddies. I suggested that we talk on the phone once a week for 30 minutes. During this weekly half-hour conversation, we would reflect on accomplishments and challenges of the week past and set goals for the week ahead. Ty and I have been partaking in this type of exchange for months. It keeps me motivated and on track. He is my witness and I am his.

Don't think this partnership happened naturally. In fact, Ty and I inhabit different worlds. He is a former Evangelical Right-Wing Christian Republican Insider who did a 180-degree turn into the world of progressive causes. The intended audience for his book, *God is Not an Elephant*, is thoughtful and/or confused Christians who, given the current political climate, are questioning their fallback political loyalties. He is married with three children, whom he and his wife are home-schooling. (They call it unschooling.) Ty holds strong Christian beliefs and lives way on the other side of town.

Contrastingly, I am a former *rebbetzin* (rabbi's wife) and a single mom with just one child who, despite much ambivalence, maintains a strong Jewish practice. I have been a supporter of liberal causes my whole life. My audience is really different than his.

Those differences aside, every conversation I have with Ty reveals more commonalities. Our conversations are rarely over in 30 minutes. We have more to talk about than just our goals as we delve more deeply into branding and who it is we really want to be. We give each other suggestions and confront each other about what we really want to be saying out in the world. He is an angel guiding me in this part of the journey. This relationship of ours is a classic Hidden Treasure—each encounter with the mutual support uncovers another little gemstone. Every experience of witnessing polishes the stone to shine a little brighter. We rarely speak for less than 60 minutes. My relationship with Ty has become a very important part of my life.

Here's the punch line: Having only met him once, a long time ago, I wouldn't recognize him if he passed me on the street,. The relationship we share is truly an unexpectedly intimate one.

The Rocket Crash and the Hidden Treasure are just two of the five broader categories I like to use to describe the idea of expectations as an important factor in rich and healthy relationships. The first three categories can be illustrated by graphing the lifecycle of different types of relationships. They are The Rocket Crash, The Altitude Adjustment, and The Hidden Treasure. The final two are Soul Mate Pie and Serendipity. This model is not a comprehensive or exhaustive one, and it hasn't been tested empirically in any formal or informal way. It is simply one perspective.

We've already talked about the Rocket Crash and Hidden Treasure. Here's what those concepts look like graphically:

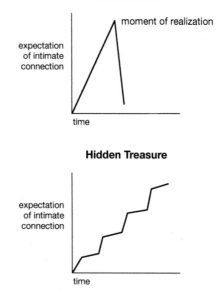

Rocket Crash

moment of realization

expectation
of intimate
connection

time

Hidden Treasure

expectation
of intimate
connection

time

The third type, the Altitude Adjustment is probably the most common trajectory in the lifecycle of relationships. You meet someone, and something about that person interests you. You get excited and imagine your connection with him or her will be bigger—more important, fulfill more needs, make your relationship life all better—than it actually is. And then you find out that affinity is not as complete as you had hoped or imagined it would be. It may start heading in the direction of the Rocket Crash, but wait .... You see that there is still some value in the connection. You just need to adjust the altitude of your expectations.

The challenge here is not to throw the proverbial baby out with the bathwater. You take a deep breath, let go of the grander expectations, and take your anticipation down a notch. At some point, in any particular relationship, you may decide that the notches have gone too low and it is no longer worth the investment of time and psychic energy to maintain the connection. But unless you reach that point, hold on... There may be a place for this relationship somewhere within your Intimacy Constellation.

Here's what the Altitude Adjustment might look like:

Altitude Adjustment

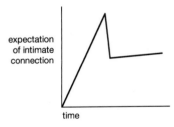

expectation
of intimate
connection

time

How big an adjustment do you need to make? Well, that depends on how much time, patience, need, and yearning you have. If the "I thought s/he was going to be my savior but isn't" relationship is really more of a tennis buddy, but I already have plenty of tennis buddies, then it might not be worth the investment. But if s/he also makes me laugh and I haven't been laughing enough lately—well then, it may just be worth adjusting the altitude and giving the relationship some time to develop.

One Particularly Big Challenge in Managing Expectations

Assumptions weaken connections. Whenever I assume something about the "other," I compromise the integrity of the web of cosmic connection. When I practice seeing beyond myself and my ideas, I know that everything is connected. In that context, I can better find my set point for my expectations.

Here's a little story. See if you can find all the assumptions and how those assumptions wreak havoc with my expectations. I'm giving you the stream-of-consciousness version so you can follow along exactly as I experienced the situation:

It happened again. Caren (not her real name) walked right by me and didn't make eye contact. I once again racked my brain to figure out what I had done to make her so uncomfortable around me that she had to ignore me like that. She and her son, Jeremy (not his real name), had been so generous to welcome our family when David started at the new school. I really thought we had made a good connection. The boys played a couple of times and Caren and I had lots of points of connection and engaged conversation. I was even hopeful that we might become friends.

Then I remembered the last conversation I'd had with Caren. I had mentioned that I had been talking to David's godmother, Dodi, about organizing a mindfulness experience for boys David's age. The aim of the activity was to give kids tools for coping with the stressful lives they experience these days. After a play date, I had mentioned to Caren that I noticed that Jeremy and David both seemed a little anxious about life stuff. I casually mentioned the mindfulness program and I wondered if she would be interested in such a program for Jeremy. She didn't seem to want to talk about it.

That must be it, I decided. I must have offended her or at least made her so uncomfortable that now she couldn't even look me in the eye. Well, that's her problem, I thought.

But still, we're going to be at this school for many years to come and it makes me so uncomfortable that she ignores me. I see her a lot at school—nearly every day, in fact, as she waits to pick up her kids.

Months go by ...

It's autumn, and that time of the year in the Jewish calendar when we are called to honestly and authentically take an accounting of our relationships and behaviors from the past year. This non-thing with Caren needs some attention.

One day, while waiting for the kids, I see her talking in a crowd of people. I nervously approach her, looking for a break in the conversation ....

"Hey, Caren. Can I talk to you for a minute?"

"Sure."

"Did I do something to offend you?"

"No! Why do you ask that?"

"It seems like you never acknowledge me when you're walking through the hallways at school or out here waiting for the kids. It has surprised me, so I thought maybe I'd done something to offend you. And now, it being Yom Kippur and all that ... well, I wanted to check in with you about it."

"Oh my God, I feel so bad. I spend so much time in my own little world that I don't notice so many things. You must think I'm so rude. I'm so embarrassed! Oh my God. I wonder how many other people I've offended like this."

Caren and I talked for another sixty minutes while our kids played on the playground. We got all caught up, during which I heard about her grad school studies and she about my growing interest in issues of human sustainability. The next time I saw her, she related how she had told her family about our conversation on the way to Yom Kippur services and thanked me again.

So much for my assumption that I had offended her.

Now, every time I see Caren, regardless of what she is doing, she meets my eyes. Sometimes we talk more. We're not close friends, yet there is now a closeness and warmth between us. With each encounter, even if it's just a smile and a wave, our hearts open, our immune systems get happy, and our souls reach out to connect.

One of the areas in which the Altitude Adjustment can be most dramatic as a strategy is with "ex" family relationships. When my ex, Jack, and I split, suddenly there was this decision point: How were we to be connected going forward? And there were also all the connections I had by virtue of my connection with him—his daughter and her children, his friends in Toronto, his sister, his new girlfriend, and on and on. After some pretty serious adjusting, Jack is very much a part of my constellation of intimate connections. The genesis of our motivation to maintain a healthy relationship may have been our son, but in the end, we both feel our lives nourished and supported by the morphed connection.

To a lesser extent, we have the opportunity to adjust anytime, even when the slightest disappointment arises. So often the disappointment is more about our own internal conversation and has nothing to do with the other player in this duo. Can we see a pattern from our past that isn't about the person we are currently connecting with but rather is about ourselves? Can we decide to respond differently this time around? Can we work on that negative self-talk, releasing, letting go, independent of the need to involve the other person in our process?

Truth be told, there are times when we just don't have it in us to do that kind of work. Then, we need to decide: Do we let the relationship fizzle or do we take our investment in it down a notch? Maybe a small and simple adjustment to our expectations is all that is necessary to do the trick.*

Soul Mate Pie

Now, don't get too excited. I am not talking about THE Soul Mate—that one who satisfies all your needs and wants—emotionally, sexually, logistically, financially—so that you can stop thinking about all this relationship stuff and just get on with your work and other important things. What I believe is that we have lots of soul mates, that we can have people in our lives who are small and big slices of our Soul Mate Pie.

For me, the defining feature of a soul mate relationship is first a sharing of heart and mind about something that is deeply valued by both individuals. This sharing is accompanied by overlapping feelings of deep understanding and satisfaction. The result is an

---

* Sometimes too much accommodating, especially if such obliging has been an ongoing unhealthy pattern, is not the way to go. And there is that "beating your head against the wall" when eventually you have to admit that things aren't changing. In short, there are times when it is right to just stop trying, especially if you suspect a rich and healthy relationship is not waiting for you at the end of the tunnel.

indescribable happiness bordering on ecstasy. These connections are not necessarily frequent or even predictable. They are often only momentary flashes, but they do occur with some regularity.

Take my friend Debbie for instance. Debbie and I are Synthesizing Soul Mates. We both can see and feel and hold paradox in a way that many people can't. We share and value a deep understanding that humans, with all our certainty, really don't know anything about anything and that at the same time, everything is connected. When we hit on those moments together, we both get really happy. Take, for example, the other day, when Debbie was telling me a story about her life and I noticed a parallel in a completely different part of existence. When I reflected on that parallel, she knew that I really understood. At that moment we both got so happy—soul mate happy.

So often the disappointment is more about our own internal conversation and has nothing to do with the other player in this duo.

I'm not the easiest person to live with and I'm sure there are some things about Debbie that would drive me crazy if we were roommates—let alone life partners. That type of incompatibility, however, doesn't stop her from being part of my Soul Mate Pie.

Then there's my friend Cindie, my Knowledge/Wisdom Soul Mate. She's one of smartest people I know, and we value and love to share thoughts and ideas. We also share a love of knowing the same small town in Costa Rica, a resonance with conscious ritual that feeds our souls, a commitment to personal growth, and the same tendency toward perfectionism. Over the years, we have witnessed each other's ups and downs, and no matter how we each are feeling about our own situation, we genuinely wish good things for the other. I question the viability of two perfectionists trying to share the same kitchen, but Cindie is undeniably part of my Soul Mate Pie.

I've had glimpses of romantic soul mate encounters that

brought up images of "this is the one"—that smart, strong, quiet Israeli man comes quickly to mind. It's too bad that, so often, romantic relationships gone awry don't retain the soul mate slice … because there is plenty of room for them.

If I had let my disappointed expectations rule, I might not be friends with either Debbie or Cindie. My friendships with these women are full and alive because I didn't throw it all away when I didn't get more than what I got. Instead, I adjusted my altitude and framed those relationships in a fresh way. And the Israeli guy? There is a thread that keeps us connected, but the soul mate nourishment was a casualty of geographically-challenged failed romance.

Here's what The Soul Mate Pie might look like:

Soul Mate Pie

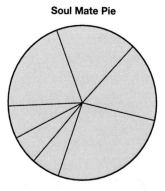

The Soul Mate Pie approach reminds me of a legend:

Whenever the shelves in the Library of Heaven were entirely full, and a new, worthy book appeared, all the books in the celestial collection pressed themselves closer together and made room.

Serendipity

All this "managing expectations" may feel a little too planned and controlled for some, especially since so many moments of connections occur seemingly by accident or chance. To cover that angle, the fifth category of expectation is Serendipity.

As an example of Serendipity, let me tell you about how I met my friends Pat and Suzanne. When we first lived in Fort Collins, on occasion Jack and I would make the pilgrimage to Denver. There were three things we'd do there that we couldn't (at that time) do in Fort Collins: eat Thai food, watch foreign films, and visit a great bookstore. On this particular occasion, I dropped Jack at the old Denver airport and headed for the Tattered Cover.

The Tattered Cover is a model independent bookstore that still thrives today. One of the special things about the Tattered Cover is the relaxed, home-like atmosphere—lots of comfy and not-so-comfy chairs in corners with old wood end tables, throw rugs, and reading lamps. Being new to Colorado, I decided to focus my time in the section with regional books. I scanned the shelves and was drawn to a book about waterfalls of Colorado—I was already feeling the dryness of this area. Quenching title in hand, I looked around to find a seat. I spotted an empty chair next to a man about my age. I noticed he was reading a book on the hot springs of Colorado. Maybe he too was feeling a bit parched? I struck up a conversation and we shared some excitement about exploring Colorado. Once we had exhausted the topic, we bade each other good-bye.

A couple months later, I bumped into this same man in the supermarket in Fort Collins. He was accompanied by his girlfriend/life partner. We immediately recognized each other and the sparks began to fly. We were so happy to see one another, that we did a little dance, right there in the middle of the grocery store. As we embraced, he gushed with the story of the hot springs he and his partner had just explored. Despite the open display of camaraderie, I didn't yet know his name.

It turned out that the pair lived in Fort Collins. I got their phone number and invited him (Pat) and his girlfriend (Suzanne) to dinner. I then went straight home to tell Jack that we had new friends—artist friends—fun, creative, imaginative new friends! (See http://www.bungledjungle.com/ for a little bit of their kind of fun.)

Our lives, up until then had been completely revolved around the Jewish community in Fort Collins, Pat and Suzanne were a notable exception to our typical social circle and a welcome addition. From the serendipitous bookstore and grocery store moments, our lives filled unexpectedly with creative artist intimacy.

Summary of Expectations

Overarching Theme

- The lifecycle of relationship is often a journey of excitement and disappointment.
- Accept yourself and other people for who they are, and embrace each relationship for what is has to offer.
- New friendship potential is everywhere. Recognize an intimate moment as an entry point.
- It's not just about new friends; it's also about deepening and strengthening connections among old friends.
- Remember that varying levels of commitment may change over time based on time availability, current needs (yours and theirs), phase in the journey, etc.

Points to Consider Regarding Expectations

It is important to distinguish between what you need, what you want, and what is available. Observe your current relationships and learn where your own strengths and pitfalls may lie. Monitor your expectations around relationships new and old.

Exercise for Expectations: Silver Lining Exercise

Bring to mind a few names of people with whom your relationship might contain some disappointment. Find what is good about this relationship.

Ask yourself: Is it enough? Can you imagine that it might be enough? Is the disappointment something that might be altered if you "check in" about it with the other? (If you do so, choose your words carefully. Don't resort to "I'm disappointed because you..." Rather, try something like "I've felt a little distance between us and I wonder if we could talk about it.")

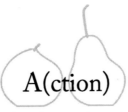

A(ction)

*Since empathy depends on emotion and since emotion is
conveyed nonverbally, to enter another's heart, you must
begin the journey by looking into his face.*

~ Daniel Pink, author, *A Whole New Mind*

THE FIRST TASK IN THE SECOND E.A.S.Y. STEP IS to determine what kind of action plan you need. You have three choices: **more, less, or different.**

More Action Plan: Can't remember the last time you went to an event or had guests to your home? Some people need to get more active; they need to get off the couch, turn off the TV, disconnect from the Internet, and get out there and meet people face to face.

Less Action Plan: Are you over-committed? Are you spread so thin that your action plan does not call for more, but rather less? If so, your best strategy may be to prioritize the thirty-seven activities you are currently involved in, pick the top seven, and go deeper rather than wider.

Different Action Plan: Stuck in a rut? Is the status quo no longer serving you? It might be that somewhere along the line you started making choices based on input and pressures from the external world. In the process, you may have put your dreams and passions first on the backburner and then into permanent storage. Or maybe you have grown emotionally, intellectually, or spiritually and outgrown the your old reliable m.o.

Take a moment and ask yourself:

- Do I need more action in my life?
- Do I need less (more focused) action in my life?
- Do I need different action in my life?

The answer to these questions will set the stage for your action plan. Regardless of which of these three groups resonate strongest for you, it is time to clarify your values. Your values will serve as your guide in the action-choosing process. More specifically, they will help you see where you want to go. That's important, because if you don't know where you want to go, it is hard to get where you want to be.

So, here's a quick exercise. Read the list of values to the right and put an asterisk (*) next to those that are highly important for you. If you have more than ten values with an asterisk, circle your top ten.

Ask yourself, "Is this something I value, from my core?"

Remember, these are *your* values. They're not what the advertising executives want you to value. They're also not what your mother/father/mentor thinks you should value. They're not even what you think you *should* value. Ask yourself, "Is this something I value, from my core?" You may want to work in pencil so you can make changes as you fine-tune your top values.

Now, make a list of all the activities you are involved in. It may be easiest to think through your week day by day, and then look at your calendar for the past month or two (and maybe even one ahead) to help complete the list. After you've finished the list, answer these three really important questions:

1) What activities are you currently involved in that speak directly to your top values? Put a check mark next to those.
2) What activities are you currently involved in that do *not* speak directly to your top values? Put an "x" next to those.
3) Which values jump out as a place of yearning for more? Put a star next to those.

Put these reflections aside. We'll get back to them later.

List Of Values
Put an asterisk (*) next to those that are important.
Circle your top 7–10.

- Accomplishments/Results
- Achievement
- Adventure/Excitement
- Aesthetics/Beauty
- Altruism
- Autonomy
- Clarity
- Commitment
- Community
- Completion
- Connecting/Bonding
- Creativity
- Emotional Health
- Environment
- Family
- Freedom
- Forward the Action
- Fun
- Honesty
- Humor
- Integrity
- Intimacy
- Joy
- Leadership
- Loyalty
- Openness
- Personal Growth/Learning
- Mastery/Excellence
- Orderliness/Accuracy
- Nature
- Partnership
- Power
- Privacy/Solitude
- Recognition/Acknowledgement
- Risk-Taking
- Romance/Magic
- Security
- Self-Expression
- Sensuality
- Service/Contribution
- Spirituality
- Trust
- Vitality

Identifying New Action Strategies

This section is filled with lots of suggestions. My best advice is to read through it, make notes of two or three strategies that jump out at you, and proceed with those that attract your attention. For example, I am much more of an "organizer" than a "joiner," so I may be more inclined to jump into action as a leader as opposed to a follower. On the other hand, if the way you've always been hasn't been working lately, you may want to stretch. In my case, joining, rather than organizing, might open up a whole new world. This process can be daunting. If you start to feel overwhelmed, take a break, go for a walk, return a phone call and come back to it with renewed energy.

The general categories of action are:

- Drop-In/Register
- Invite
- Volunteer
- Join
- Organize

As you move through the list of suggestions, keep your values in mind.

#1 Register/Drop-In

For people who need more or different strategies, this action category is the lowest risk strategy for expanding or deepening social opportunities. People who need less should feel free to read this section, being careful to add more deeply but not more widely.

About Meetup.com

If you are looking for more or different strategies for social connections, you ought to know about meetup.com. Meetup.com is a social networking site that aptly states on its home page, "Use the Internet to get off the Internet." People who want to meet others who share their interests can join one of the listed groups or start their own. Although the groups organize online, all ensuing activity is conducted face to face.

As a newcomer to meetup.com, you can enter your zip code and choose a radius. You can then see what groups are meeting in your area. When I put in my zip code and a ten-mile radius, 434 groups are listed. When I expand to twenty-five miles, the number of groups increases to 803.

You love sports photography? There are ninety-three others, in my "neighborhood," who have registered to meet up about that topic. Or what about ping pong (eighty-two members)? In these political times, there are 153 Libertarians and five groups for Democrats, including "Young Democrats Happy Hour" with 225 members. I, myself, am registered in one of the many walking groups (ninety-three members), the Idea Café (224 members) and the theatre goers meet up (311 members).

"What?" you may be thinking, 311 people are going to the theater together? Not exactly. People are busy. Very often the event that the organizer—an ordinary person like you or me—has planned isn't convenient for 97% of the people who are registered. So, what that means is that maybe only nine people meet up for the identified performance and seven people show up to the Idea Café. And at the next event, it may be nine and seven different people.

Meetup.com is notorious as a changing community. The meetings themselves are not necessarily the place to evolve lasting relationships, but they are a place to network (try identifying one person at the meeting you want to meet-up with again), to feel part of something bigger than yourself, and to open yourself up to more possibilities. Some meet-ups do form a core of closer-knit groups, and they can be a place to make connections that become deeper relationships. (See story inset on page 198.)

In most communities, there are numerous "Drop-in" opportunities: exercise classes, art classes, library-sponsored book groups, city-sponsored gardening classes. All of these opportunities are low risk and at low or no cost.

Moving to a slightly higher level of risk, let's take a look at the idea of registering for a class. As a committed, lifelong learner, I am constantly taking classes. Here in Denver, we have Colorado Free University (CFU). It isn't exactly free—most classes run $39–$49 for a three-hour session—but with a bit of budgeting consciousness, it is affordable for many individuals. Most cities have their own brand of inexpensive adult education classes. The only downside is that a little higher risk is involved. That's because if the class is a bomb, you can feel like you wasted a precious chunk of time and you're out the $50 bucks.

I've registered for classes ranging from "Tie One On" (scarf tying) to "How to Sell Your Book on the Radio." The next one I'm pining for is tree climbing for grown-ups. Of course, the possibilities are endless—art, improv, HTML, foreign language, parenting, investing, dancing, yoga, fencing, real estate, writing … take your pick. In

Serendipity à la Meetup

A couple years ago, I registered for the Denver Spanish Conversation Meet-up. There are groups speaking Spanish together every Monday and Wednesday evening around the Denver Metro area. For two and half hours the people who gather speak only Spanish. Most of the meetings, it turns out, are held quite a distance from my house, and always from 7:30 to 10:00 p.m. As a result, they conflict with my important role as mother at bedtime on school nights.

Every week, I would get the notice that a group of Spanish speakers was meeting, but I never went. Then I had an idea. What if I hosted a meet-up at my home?! Now, on the second Monday of each month, between ten and fifteen of the 1,081 people registered for the Spanish Conversation meet-up arrive at my front door.* The group is composed of a small core of returning conversationalists, most of whom live nearby and come most months. As a nice change of pace, there are always new people.

One of the returning people is Ricardo. Ricardo and I very quickly realized we had a lot in common—we are both Jewish, both divorced at the same time, both have kids around the same age, and both have a good relationship with our ex-family. Furthermore, we both like tennis (haven't played together yet) and both have strong connections to Costa Rica. Ricardo also made a nice connection with David. I've had him here at my home for dinner, and he's invited me back to his. We speak on the phone maybe once a month in addition to seeing each other at Spanish. It's not romantic. Rather, it is a brotherly/sisterly kind of friendship.

---

* A note on safety: In order to feel comfortable inviting people I didn't know to my house, I asked a friend to come to the first one and stay until everyone had left.

fact, I met my Hidden Treasure friend Ty at a class at CFU.

Not all registration is low risk. You could sign up for a conference, a retreat, or a vacation, and depending on the price and length of time, the risk could get pretty high. Of course, increased risk means there is also the possibility of higher rewards, so consider the tradeoff.

> **Action Possibility #1:**
> Pick one low-risk activity that you imagine you would enjoy. Drop-in or Register today!

#2 Invite

I have three rules I follow when it comes to invitations:

1) Be bold (don't be afraid to make the first move);

2) Set cautious expectations (protect yourself from the Rocket Crash); and

3) Don't take rejection personally. (People are busy. That's life in the 21st century.)

A few years ago, my son David and I moved to a just-right house in an old (for Colorado) neighborhood. The first thing my sweet father did was send me a check for $250 with a note that read, "Have your neighbors over." Following his advice, I hosted an elegant "just desserts" gathering. Thirty-five neighbors came, and by the end of the evening, everyone was buzzing about who would host the next one. (I'm planning to do another one—this time potluck.) Now, when I walk in my neighborhood, I have so many people to chat with. As a result of my neighborly hospitality I feel very much like I belong.

Be bold. Get on the phone or send an email, and invite someone you like or want to get to know better to something ... anything. Here in Denver, we have 1st Fridays, where all the art galleries in one area of town open their doors to the public. On the first Friday of every month, year round, they serve refreshments to patrons. Also, all summer long, free concerts take place all around the city. These are just two examples.

If you happen to be one of the more industrious, invite people to your house for a meal— maybe Sunday brunch or Saturday dinner. Robert Putnam, in his book *Bowling Alone*, reports that the act of having a friend over or going out with friends is on a dramatic declining plane. The data show that in 1975, Americans, on average, entertained in the home 14 to 15 times per year. By 1999, that number had declined by 45%.

Putnam goes on to report that family picnics have nearly vanished. What's that about? Two-income families with no time to clean house? People too overwhelmed by the volumes of email and errands to keep a household going? Kids over-committed with sports and recitals? Too much TV and Internet?

I am committed to swimming against this current. We are connected with a couple of families with whom we alternate hosting duties—they come here, then a couple months later we go there, and a couple more months pass and they come here again. These regular meet-ups keep us in the flow of each others' busy lives. I always keep it simple—hummus appetizer with soup or stew and salad. I ask guests to bring dessert. Sometimes we play games or watch movies. More often, the kids play and the grown-ups just hang out together in leisure conversation. I admit that I do most of the reminding that it's time to schedule another get-together. As a small investment with a big payoff, the effort is more than worth it.

> **Action Possibility #2:**
> Be bold. Make a stew. Invite someone over.

#3 Volunteer

We could have a longer discussion about whether inviting is riskier than volunteering. For me, the factor that makes the difference is the length of time commitment. I usually think of volunteering as a longer commitment than inviting. Maybe that's because when I volunteer to tutor adults who are learning to speak English as a foreign language, I have to take training classes and commit to a schedule. That feels riskier than inviting a new friend over for soup and salad.

The most important thing to consider when choosing a place to volunteer is that it resonates with your values. Go back to the list of values and review it often as you make decisions about where to spend your time. Expect to give more than you receive and then stay open to Serendipity. Pick one cause and stick with it for years to maximize this kind of benefit, or dabble around if you are still finding your place. You might also consider inquiring at your place of work or worship about volunteer opportunities. Often, those environments have identified a charitable organization for their community to rally around.

Here are just a few places you may want to consider if volunteering is on the list of things you want to do to expand your social connections:

- Neighborhood associations
- Habitat for Humanity
- Local events
- Nursing home
- Soup kitchen
- Food bank
- Habitat clean-up
- Animal shelter
- Disabled assistance
- Symphony
- Literacy
- Museum
- Local school
- Kids a risk
- Board of directors of a non-profit
- Political issue group
- Church
- Professional organization
- Civic organization
- Hospitals
- Immigrants
- Seniors
- Specific disease/cure
- Conflict resolution
- Library
- Environmental/conservation

Need more guidance? Many cities have a centralized organization that can match you with volunteer opportunities.

Action Possibility #3:
Pick one thing from the list of volunteer opportunities that jumps out at you. Make a call and ask, "How can I help?"

#4 Join

Even though "join" is riskier for me than "organize," I recognize that for the majority of the people it is the other way around. Join a group where your values shine.

Two characteristics that distinguish joining from registering or inviting are the nature of the group and the level of investment. While the groups in question can be for work or play, for intellectual stimulation or exercise, or affiliated religiously or professionally, their identity does not revolve around a one-time activity. Rather, any group you join will have a shared common goal, interest, or vision. Often, as one of its members, you will be asked to make a commitment that furthers the group's mission. As a result, you are less able to remain anonymous. I view joining as a higher risk than volunteering not only because of the increased investment, but also because by joining, you make a statement to the world about your affiliation. By joining, you declare, "I want to belong here."

Some common groups that people join, hoping to find connection, are:

- Book discussion groups
- Play groups
- Religious institutions
- Civic organizations (e.g., Rotary, Kiwanis, Lions)
- Professional associations
- Martial arts practice
- Performing arts
- Special interest groups (e.g., master gardening, race car, etc.)
- Co-housing

Action Possibility #4:
Consult your values. Join a group where your values shine.

#5 Organize

The goal of organizing is to bring people together. I've been organizing since I was a young child—when my sisters and I would hold a neighborhood fair, selling our old comic books, hawking lemonade, and telling fortunes with our magic eight ball. We donated the proceeds to The American Cancer Society.

Forty-five years later, I'm still doing neighborhood organizing. A few months ago, motivated by my own desire to do yoga every day, I sent out an "Interest Survey" in the monthly home owners' association newsletter. In it, I listed all kinds of interests including crafts, games, lecture series, movement, book discussion, movies, cooking, sports, and yoga among them. The idea of the survey is that I will let whoever submits a response know who else in the neighborhood shares that interest. I'm even offering to convene the first meeting for a group if no one else in that group has stepped up to the plate to organize. I suggested that rather than sitting in front of the TV or taking a long drive to meet people, we can save gas, get some exercise, and meet people in our own backyard.

It can be especially rewarding to organize within one of the groups where you volunteer or have joined. Recall the story "*Hajimete* Meets Jewish Women" and how that bond among the Rosh Hodesh women deepened the commitment to the wider Jewish community. All it took was a little organizing—establishing a process, giving some thought to the content, and getting it on the calendar. Then, the "Be Bold" kicks in, inviting people to check it out. Of course, there are more details—making sure the room is set, the heat is on, there are some refreshments and that moving forward, there is a way for people to stay in touch.

Action Possibility #5:
If you have organizational skills, share them. People always appreciate the effort. If you've never done so, give it try. Start small and find a buddy to co-organize so the prospect isn't so daunting.

A(ction) Summary

Overarching Themes

There are three kinds of people who may require change in the world of social connections: those who need more action, those who need less (or more focused) action, and those who need a different path to get them to the desired levels of social connection.

Target Resources Wisely

Any change is risky. How much risk do you want to handle? Do you want to flow or do you want to stretch?

The Big Obstacle to Action

I'm not going to mince words here. Excuses limit success.

My house is too messy, I'm too old, I don't have enough experience, I'm too tired, it's too late, it's too early, I can't afford it, I don't have time.

I'm not saying that some of these things aren't true, but if you hear yourself making excuses, play the devil's advocate—challenge yourself or shift the setup so it'll work for you.

Take, for example, my Spanish group. It was too far, so I brought it to my house. Another example: My mother, who doesn't drive at night, was balking at registering for an art class that meets from 1:00 to 5:00 in the afternoon because it would start getting dark by the time the class was over. When she realized she could just leave early when it started getting too dark, that made all the difference. Even being too tired is no excuse. Studies have shown that moderate fatigue is relieved by movement, not by sitting in front of the TV, which in and of itself is fatiguing.

Likewise, your house doesn't have to be spic 'n span to have company over for a visit. Gone is the era when we all had the time to keep house like June Cleaver in *Leave it to Beaver*. Pick up in one room, spend five minutes with a rag in the bathroom, and get over it. Your friends will be so happy to be invited that they won't even notice the pile of clothes you threw into the closet.

Action Exercise

If you determined that your path to action is either **more or different**, name one to three actions (register, invite, volunteer, join, or organize) you would want to take if you had more time. Be sure to keep your list of values front and center, choosing an activity or group that honors the best of your values. Then, put it on the calendar and make the time. (To support your success with this endeavor, read the section on Choice and Change, pages 229–232.)

If you determined that **less** is the theme of the next steps, identify one to two places where you want to invest more, one to two activities you are going to stop, and one to two commitments where you are going to cut back. (By the way, these numbers are totally arbitrary and ought to be set to reflect your actual experience. If you are currently involved in 40 projects, the numbers may need to be a littler higher. If you are involved in five, they may be smaller.) Be sure to keep your list of values front and center. For more support to actually get this endeavor done, read the section on Choice and Change, pages 229–232.

S(ocial Lubrication)

Please! Sit here by the stove.
It gives a good warmth—just as you.

~ Tsurukichi Seki Ainu, island of Hokkaido, Japan,
Inviting a guest into his home

WHETHER I AM DIRECTLY ENGAGED IN A conversation or watching from the sidelines, I have made it a practice to observe how people talk with one another. In the process, I've noticed four different styles of conversation. Each has its own set of pros and cons, so I don't present them here with any judgment.

Well, let me be completely honest...

I don't have a judgment about the styles of conversation—as each style definitely has its place in the development of relationship. However, I do make a judgment about the lack of consciousness many people have around the use of styles. My intention is to shine some light on this subject.

The four styles of conversation I regularly observe are:

- Parallel Conversation
- Points of Connection Conversation
- Engaged Conversation
- Revealing/Deep Listening Conversation

Parallel Conversation
Like parallel play, parallel conversation looks like this: I say something about my life, such as, "My book group decided to read old favorites this year. We are starting with Marge Piercy's *He, She and It.*" Then you say something about your life, such as, "The Farmers' Market had the juiciest organic peaches. I bought a dozen this week."

So, let's look at what happened. In addition to the me-centered pleasure of telling whoever is around me about my life, I have also given you a recommendation for a great read. Similarly, you have given me the idea to get myself to the farmers' market. There is nothing wrong with this conversation. In fact, it can serve to keep people who are already in a relationship connected. In a large group, it can serve as a way of checking in or updating so that everyone can feel as though they belong. Its limitations are that it rarely deepens or strengthens connections.

Points of Connection Conversation
It might look like this: I say, "The Farmers' Market had the juiciest organic peaches. I bought a dozen this week." Then you say, "Me too! The juice ran down my arm." Encouraging more points of connections, you may follow that with, "Did you taste that pesto from the new dipping sauce vendor?"

This style of conversation is "me too!" centered. It is great for helping people who may not know one another that well feel connected to each other. It can serve to highlight shared interests that can, in turn, lead to making plans to spend more time together. "Hey, wanna meet at the Market next week?" would be a fine active end to this Points of Connection conversation.

Engaged Conversation
By far my favorite, engaged conversation is one where all participants remain on one related topic until a new depth of understanding and connection has been explored. This type of conversation moves back and forth and is infused with curiosity and sustained attention. Each participant, rather than simply contributing his or her own thoughts to the conversation, reflects and deepens the thoughts of others who are engaged in the conversation.

In some ways, the content is less important than the process. Engaged conversation calls on all parties to stay in the place of curiosity, to share, and to be willing to set aside any expectations of their contributions being the center of attention. It is a collaborative experience, and with each contribution, the shared experience grows.

I always keep three good "small talk"* questions in my hip pocket to jumpstart Engaged Conversations so they stay engaged.

1) When meeting a new person: "What is your connection to this person/place/event?"
2) When reconnecting with someone I don't know well: "Are you still involved with … ?" If the response is yes, follow with, "What's new with [it]?" If the response is no, follow with, "So how have filled that time?"
3) When reconnecting with some I know well: "How are you feeling about … ?"

A few years ago, I was a guest at a Dialogue Group. Having already confessed to you that Engaged Conversation is my favorite sport, and given that this group had been "doing dialogue" for many years, I was anticipating the meeting like a new mother awaits the birth of her first child. I perceived it as a whole evening of conscious engaged dialogue! In my mind's eye, I saw it as a deepening of connection to both topic and people, a virtual slice of heaven.

Sadly, I was in for a disappointment. I soon discovered that although this group claimed years of experience in the practice of dialogue, there were no ground rules and that people pretty much said whatever they felt like saying at any given moment. Instead of dialogue with deepening connections, what I witnessed was three hours of look-at-me parallel talk. Honestly, I don't remember the content of the conversation, but imagine if the topic had been "How might we support people to live more sustainable lives?" The parallel conversation that day would have sounded something like this:

"I think the FDA needs a complete re-haul, because our food system is out of control."

"That may be, but what about exercise? The obesity rate just keeps increasing."

"I read a great book about global warming."

---

* See Debra Fine's The Art of Small Talk for more strategies.

"People just need more willpower. They should be teaching willpower in the schools."

"It reminds me of the time I had this experience …"

"What about China? They have billions of people who want everything we have."

"Has anyone tried the quiche?"

Now, taken out of context, each comment would make for a great conversation. But taken in sequence … not once in three hours did one person's comment take the conversation deeper. I felt like I was in the look-at-me twilight zone.

The definition of a dialogue is "a discussion between two or more people or groups, especially one directed toward an exploration of a particular subject or resolution of a problem."*

On Planet Sarah, a dialogue group would have some ground rules:

1) The conversation would start with a general question, such as, "How might we support people to live more sustainable lives?"

2) The first person to speak on the topic sets the theme for the next five, six, or seven comments—or more. She might say, "Shouldn't we first define sustainability? I think it goes way beyond the first thought of environmentalism."

3) The next four to six comments need to stay on this topic (what we mean when we talk about sustainability). Each subsequent comment must be must be related to what the previous comment addressed.

Looking at the Model Dialogue on the right, do you notice anything unusual in this conversation? There's no "look at me" or "me too" contributions. Instead, there is connection to the topic, attention to what others have to say, and curiosity about how the conversation unfolds. The engagement of each speaker and the listeners is palpable.

---

* Mac OS 10.4.11 dashboard dictionary

Model Engaged Dialogue

The topic is introduced: "How might we support people to live more sustainable lives?"

Make sure everyone is talking about the same thing: "Shouldn't we first define sustainability? I think it goes way beyond the first thought of environmentalism."

The conversation might continue: "I agree. I always loved when George Carlin said that we don't have to save the planet. The planet is doing just fine. We have to save humans on the planet."

"I think that as we define sustainability, we need to look more at systems. You know, how Al Gore says we are borrowing money from China to pay the Saudis for oil that we use to pollute our environment and that the whole system has to change."

"Similarly, we could say that about the transportation system, the health care system, and the food system—like how food manufacturers are producing "food products" that are refined to the point that they are stripped of nutritional value and essential omega-3 fat so they can be transported far away and stay "fresh" (not go rancid) on a shelf for a long time. We could say that the whole system needs to change."

"I don't know about the omega-3 story. Can someone say more about that?"

"Well, we evolved from creatures of the sea, and when we finally settled on land, we still ate mostly from the sea. All those foods—fish and seaweed and the wild grasses that grow on the shores—are all high in omega-3 fat, which is critical for our brains to develop. The problem is that is gets rancid very quickly so it can't be used in processed foods. Basically, any food you buy from the center aisles at the grocery store has no omega-3"

"So there might be one strategy for helping people live more sustainably. Get them to shop only on the outside of the store. I'll start a list."

"Can we put books on the list, too? Can anyone recommend a good book to read more about omega-3?

"*The Omnivore's Dilemma*, by Michael Pollen"

"That's a great book. I especially liked the chapter on the grass farmer. He really told the whole story in the chapter."

"Why was that chapter so special?"...

Revealing/Deep-Listening Conversation
Some people ask, "What is the difference between sharing and revealing?" Sharing is providing information; revealing is expressing how you feel about that information. Here's a good example from my own life. I was married for fifteen years to a rabbi. I've just shared a piece of information. But there is more to that for me. Being married to a rabbi was not always easy. Often, I felt objectified as "The Rabbi's Wife" and sensed that very few people cared to know the real me.

In the first case, by telling you I was a *rebbetzin*, I open the conversation to points of connection and even engagement. With the second statement, I send out a spark of authenticity, providing fuel to deepen the roots of our connection. I let you get to know me.

Revealing is a little like getting naked, and like nudity, it isn't appropriate for every connection. It is, however, required for the deepest and strongest relationships. It is only when you bare all that you reach the deepest plane of connectivity.

Four Rules of Social Lubrication on Planet Sarah
In Japanese culture, the rules of social etiquette are formal and culturally ingrained. When I first encountered the Japanese concepts of obligation,* I thought of them as a burden. I mean, with my Western brain, burden felt like part of the definition of obligation. Now I see it differently. In our crazy busy 21st-century lives, where we are so overwhelmed that we can hardly take time for the reflection we need to prioritize with integrity, a little formalized cultural expectation might just be a relief.

On Planet Sarah—if I were in charge—there would be four basic rules of social etiquette: Introduce, Respond, Reciprocate, and Step Aside.

1. Introduce
In Japan, an introduction carries weight. People don't introduce themselves; rather, they count on a third party to make an intro-

---

* The Japanese words are *giri* and *on* and are difficult to translate. Check the Internet or find a book on Japanese culture if you are interested to learn more.

duction. This third party is responsible for far more than just revealing names and initiating small talk. On a spiritual level, he or she is charged with the evolution of the relationship. For example, when two people get married, the person who introduced them is given the seat of honor. Weeks, months or years after being introduced, when two people have conflict in their relationship, they call upon the introducer for counsel or even to intervene. This formal setup creates a cohesion—a web of social connections—that adds strength and safety to Japanese society.

For better or worse, we have nothing like this introductory formality in our American culture. We have only what we informally call "social networks," where we may call upon people we know to introduce us to others. What gets lost with this informality is a consciousness around the act of making everyday introductions. In fact, sometimes it doesn't happen at all. The consequence is people feeling lost or left out. This simple act of formally introducing two people can change everything.

To learn more about this dichotomy, I decided to watch one of the experts in the field of social connection. My son, David, is one of the most social beings I know. I've learned a lot from watching him in his first twelve years of life. Because he is innately gregarious, David learns social cues quickly and takes social counsel easily. From early on, I suggested that when he is in a situation with a friend who is not known to others, he make introductions. This socialization approach is now second nature for him.

Last week, as we were leaving the house in the car to drive David's friend Ben home, we passed our neighbor, who also happens to be the librarian at David's school. She had recently lent me a (powerful) book (*The Book Thief*), and I stopped to thank her and to strengthen our connection. While we chatted, she looked into the back seat and saw David and Ben.

David said, "Ms. Bush, this is my friend Ben."

"Hi, Ben. Where do you go to school?" she inquired.

A brief conversation ensued. The moment was simple yet full of friendship, respect, and warm feelings that boosted our immune systems. It was a beautiful thing to watch two new souls connecting right in front of our eyes.

So next time you find yourself standing in a group where not everyone knows everyone, be bold. Make the introductions.

2. Respond

RSVP comes from the French for "please respond." What used to be understood as common courtesy is no longer common. Internet technology has made wide and rapid communication so much more accessible, and as a result, new rules for have begun to develop. Unfortunately, we haven't been so thoughtful or formal about these new rules. Not all of them support stronger connections. Some tear at the very fabric of our need for human connection; others are just plain rude.

For example, let's look at the online job application process. I've been self-employed since 1982, but I recently thought about looking for employment. The rationale behind this shift in thinking was to connect my human sustainability work with something larger than my own small consulting business. To that end, I registered my areas of interest on a few of the websites that allow you to check off all the types of jobs that might be a good match for you. Now when positions open in any related area, the system automatically emails the job post to me.

One day, a listing for a Health Educator popped up and I thought, "Why not?" Later, I found that same listing on Craigslist and on the Colorado Non-Profit Job Board. I Googled the phrase and location and found numerous listings on the Internet. How many résumés do you think that employer got? 500? 5,000? According to one source in the recruitment industry, the latter is more likely than the former. What is it like, as a recruiter, to have to weed through 5,000 applications? And what, then, is the experience of being one of those 5,000?

It used to be that when you applied for a job, you would either get a letter thanking you for your interest but declining to move forward, or you would get a phone call to set up an interview. Either way, there was a connection. Today, organizations state up front that you should not expect even an acknowledgment that they have received your résumé. The underlying message is that they will contact you (when?) if they are interested. As a result, the job seeker is in a perpetual state of limbo.

I don't blame the prospective employers. They are just people and they are overwhelmed by the 5,000 notes in their inbox. Applicants with unusual or diverse backgrounds who might be just what these hiring organizations need (like me!) are likely out on the first round. That's because they often to don't have all the standard keywords that are being used to cull the pile.

This is the downside of technology. It has birthed a whole new pathway of disconnection.

Now, whereas I can bring myself to acknowledge and even appreciate the space between the rock and the hard place of the above scenario, what I don't understand is people who don't reply to individual, personal email. It hasn't happened to me that often, but I have many reports from loads of people. They send emails and the recipient doesn't respond. My first reaction is to be confused. Did they not get my email? Others, who are more used to this feel discouraged or angry. To me, this lack of response is like passing someone on the street, waving, saying "hello," and having that person make no acknowledgment that you have sent friendly energy in their direction.

Don't they know that to ignore is to set in motion a disruption of the cosmic web? My guess is that they don't. More likely, their motivation (or lack thereof) is guilt, conflict avoidance, or plain and simple crazy busy 21st-century overwhelm.

Once, I actually applied for a job where I was contacted for an interview. The business was owned by a partnership of two young men. I was interviewed for 90 minutes by one partner and then asked to "audition" for the job. That process entailed about ten hours of work over one week, during which the aim was to create a mock proposal using the company's business model. This audition was followed by another ninety-minute interview to review the created proposal, this time by both partners. At the end the second interview, when I inquired about next steps, the second partner told me that the first would be in touch by the end of the week. One week passed with no correspondence and I sent a note to inquire with the first. In his quick reply, he indicated some confusion between partners and assured me that he would get back to me shortly. I never heard from him again.

That type of neglect is just plain rude, but my guess is that he wasn't maliciously motivated. He and I had made a good connection during that first interview. We had also interacted a number of times (all positive, even flattering) during the week I was working on the proposal. My guess is that after all the hard work I put in, the idea of contacting me to let me know that they were *not* going to extend an offer of employment was just too uncomfortable a scenario for the young man. The consequence of having no formal societal rule requiring a response is that I spent a couple of extra weeks in jobseeker limbo. More critically though is that the young man did not have to face me, and as a result lost the opportunity for personal and professional growth.

While emotional immaturity accounts for a significant chunk of non-response, let's not underestimate the significance of 21st-century overwhelm. A 2006 estimate of the number of non-spam emails sent daily was 25 billion. Oh My G!d. The ramifications of these statistics, combined with employers' expectations that people will get more done than ever in their work day, are almost incomprehensible. Many people simply do not have time.

I'm not suggesting that everyone has to invest in every relationship. Sometimes it just becomes too much and we have to set limits. That's healthy. Still, I'd like to suggest that there can be some automatic responses that can be employed in the healthiest of ways—ways that do *not* disrupt the cohesion of the cosmic web— that still allow each of us to be sane. What we need are thoughtful and acceptable I-can't-possibly-deal-with-this-right-now" responses. For example:

Receiver's Possible Replies
A) If you have been subscribed to a listserv that no longer serves you, and there is no easy unsubscribe button, you could send the following message:

Dear Friends,
In an effort to simplify my life, I am on an email diet—cutting back on email subscriptions. Please help me by removing this

email address from your list.
Thanks for understanding,
Your Name

B) If you are so overwhelmed that you can hardly look at your email, but the message is from someone with whom you want to maintain a connection, you could send the following reply. The beauty of this strategy is that you can implement it without even reading the note from the sender:

Dear Friend,
I am up to my eyeballs in email and I can't even predict when I'll have time to read your note. If it is urgent, please call me at ...
Thanks for understanding,
Your Name

or

Dear Friend,
The abundance of life is making it difficult to keep up with email but I wanted to let you know that I got yours. If it is urgent, please resend with "Urgent" in the subject line. Otherwise, I'll get back to you within [a reasonable time period].
Thanks for understanding,
Your Name

C) If the sender is someone with whom you have no interest in continuing a relationship, you can still avoid rudeness. In the process, you can save the universe from more tears in the cosmic web by clearly responding:

Dear Friend,
I got your note/request/idea/proposal/communication. I have too much on my plate to be able to respond/engage/consider anything more.
Thanks for understanding and best of luck.
Your Name

D) Finally, you may want to consider sending the following message in response to any emails where the passage of time may result in a better/more thoughtful communication:

Dear Friend,
I got your note and it deserves my full attention. I'd like to take some time to reflect on it. I'll get back to you in [a reasonable time period].
Thanks for understanding,
Your Name

Sender's Expectations

As the sender, you can also be thoughtful about clearly stating what kind of action you are expecting. For example, you could state up front:

1) *No reply is needed.*
2) *Please confirm receipt. No further action is needed.*
3) *Please reply with one of the following statements:*
   a) I have read and I am ready to move forward.
   b) I have some questions before I can move forward.
   c) I'm not sure I have time/resources to commit/respond to this right now.
   d) I haven't had time to read it yet, but will get back to you [insert date].
4) *Here's my news. I'd love to hear back from you, but I also know how busy everyone is. Don't feel bad if you don't have time to reply. Know that I'll still like/love you anyway.*

Alternatively, you could send that ultimatum statement:

5) *If I don't hear by … I'll assume you are not interested.*

3. Reciprocate

This, the third rule on Planet Sarah, reminds me of Robert Fulghum's book, *All I Really Need to Know I Learned in Kindergarten.*

- When someone smiles at you, smile back.
- When someone invites you to dinner, invite them back.
- When someone makes a personal or professional connection for you, connect them back.
- When someone sends you a gift, give them a verbal or written thank you.
- When someone pays you a random act of kindness, either pay it back or pay it forward.
- Oh, and I almost forgot. An important part of the reciprocate rule is not to assume that the next generation learns by osmosis. Teach these lessons to the next generation.

4. Step Aside

Cell phones have entered our society at an unprecedented rate of speed. Today, there are more cellular subscribers than land-line phone subscribers in the world. In the United Kingdom, there are more mobile phones than people in the country. The Gartner Group predicts that one billion mobile phones will be sold worldwide in the year 2009.

I recently went for a walk with a friend. A few minutes into our time together, her phone rang. She said, "Oh, I've been waiting for a call from A." She then looked at the caller ID and said, "Hmmm ... I don't know who that is." Nevertheless, she proceeded to answer.

It wasn't A and it wasn't important, but nonetheless, for the next five minutes, she and I walked while she talked to some unimportant person on the phone. If she interrupted our time together to talk with that unimportant person, how important did she think I felt? My guess is that she was not thinking.

Later that day, I was at the grocery store in the checkout line. It's one of those lines where everyone stands together and there are five cashiers. Each one's little station lights up when he or she becomes available. Suddenly, the woman in front of me got a call. She answered and chatted away, not noticing when it was her turn to move into the line. As a result, the system came to a grinding halt.

Don't these people know that they are disrupting the cohesion of the cosmic web? Is this not the perfect opportunity to bring mindfulness to bear on the impact of our actions on the world around us?

I suggest four simple rules of cell phone etiquette:

1. If you are on your own, out in a public place, your cell phone rings, and you decide to answer it, step aside.
2. If you are with people and are expecting a call, let them know that your time together may be interrupted. When/if the call comes, excuse yourself and step aside.
3. If you are with people, the phone rings, and it is the nurse at your son's school or it's some other call you are compelled to take, apologize to your company. Let them know that the call is critical, then excuse yourself and step aside.
4. If you are with people—and this includes standing in a checkout line—the phone rings, and the call is not urgent, it's just plain rude to answer it. That's what voicemail is for.

In the event you do need to take a call in public, for G!d's sake, keep your voice down.

Find a Way to Reach Out

Social Lubrication, then, is about respect, attention, and authenticity. In the end, developing strong and deep relationships takes time. Consider the following story:

In the *New York Times*' Op-Ed section on June 23, 2008, I read a story by Peter Lovenheim. Peter lived in a small suburban community in upstate New York. One day, a tragic event took place in Peter's neighborhood: A man shot and killed his wife and then turned the gun on himself. Their two middle-school age children ran screaming from the house. Soon afterward, a "for sale" sign went up. Nothing had changed ... except for Peter.

It distressed Peter how little had changed—how little this tragedy that had occurred just doors away in the house of his neighbor of seven years had affected his life and the life of his family. He asked the question, "Why is it that in an age of cheap long-distance rates, discount airlines, and the Internet, when we can create community anywhere, we often don't know the people who live next door?" It didn't seem like the way humans were meant to live, and Peter decided to change it.

Looking back on his childhood, it occurred to him that the way he best got to know people was by hanging out at their homes and sleeping over. He began to ask his neighbors if he could do precisely that. About half of them declined his request but the other half agreed, and thus the sleepovers began. Much to the embarrassment of his teen at home, Peter could regularly be seen leaving his home with a small overnight bag slung over his shoulder, on his way to the neighbor's house.

Often sleeping in the room of a child who had grown up and left home, Peter had a treasure chest of conversation pieces at his fingertips. Sharing breakfast and the morning routine, he would hear stories of family histories, and by the end of the day, he would witness both laughter and tears. In some cases, he found a neighbor in need and brought others together to help. The research tells us that the safest neighborhoods are those where people know each other. For Peter, it just made him feel human.

In his final reflection, Peter said, "Our political leaders speak of crossing party lines to achieve greater unity. Maybe we should all cross the invisible lines between our homes and achieve greater unity in the places we live. Probably we don't need to sleep over; all it might take is to make a phone call, send a note, or ring a bell. Why not try it today?"

Y(ou in the Universe)

"I am like a falling star who has finally found her place next to another in a lovely constellation, where we will sparkle in the heavens forever."

~ Amy Tan, American writer and novelist

DO YOU KNOW WHAT HAPPENS IN THIS LAST step of the E.A.S.Y. process? You get to be at the center of your universe. Yes, you ... no one else ... you.

All around you are points of light—people who are in your life on a daily, weekly, seasonally, or sporadic basis. The connections with these beings provide nourishment for your own soul. As a result, your connection with them nourishes their souls.

If I were to ask you to list the people with whom you have intimate connections, how many would there be? Five? Ten? Twenty? My guess is that there are more than you think there are. In fact, my goal is to see if I can help you find them. This is your chance to put pencil to paper and bring your Intimacy Constellation to life.

The first thing to do is make a list of all the people with whom you feel you have an intimate connection. At this point, we are defining intimacy broadly and generously—an intimate moment as in any time one person sees, hears, understands, or witnesses another, and an intimate relationship as one in which intimate moments are shared over time. At some point, you may want to rein in your definition—take some of the people off the list as not really members of intimate relationships. But for now, for the sake of being open, broaden the circle.

To help get the brain cells working, use the list of "Intimacy Types" as a springboard. It is by no means comprehensive or exhaustive list; it simply provides some guidance through the physical, emotional, intellectual, and spiritual possibilities of intimate connection. Feel free to add your own categories.

Categories of Intimate Connection
Reading through these categories may help you to generate a list of people with whom you have intimate connections.

- Fun-Loving Intimacy
- Activity Intimacy (specific/general)
- Financial Intimacy (e.g., accountant)
- Physical Space Intimacy (e.g., carpool)
- Sexual Intimacy
- Humorous Intimacy
- Gastronomical Intimacy
- Musical Intimacy
- Romantic Intimacy
- Recreational Intimacy
- Conversational Intimacy
- Sisterly Emotional Intimacy
- Brotherly Emotional Intimacy
- Fatherly Emotional Intimacy
- Motherly Emotional Intimacy
- Spousal Emotional Intimacy
- Interpersonal Emotional Processing Intimacy
- Intrapersonal Emotional Processing Intimacy
- General Interpersonal Emotional Intimacy
- Educational Intimacy
- Professional Intimacy
- Career Path Intimacy
- Vocational Intimacy (specific)
- Neighborly Intimacy
- Celebration and Ritual Intimacy
- Philosophical Intimacy
- Religious Intimacy
- Being Intimacy
- Spiritual Intimacy

Don't worry if you think you don't completely understand a category. There are no strict rules about what belongs. If the sense of intimacy is shared among a group rather than with individuals (such as a religious community), list the group. Pets are also okay.

Experiences, too. Like I said, at this point, be generous. At the same time, you don't need to "complete" the list. By definition, this list is a work-in-progress—a snapshot of life as it is today. You will have more opportunities to add to it later and revisit it whenever you want.

So, go ahead. Make your list right now. I'll wait.

Got your list? Take a moment to take it in. So rarely in our busy 21st-century lives do we allow ourselves time for reflection. Although reflection is critical for our emotional health and spiritual growth, it has become what is seen as a luxury. Look at each name on your list and feel gratitude for all the nourishment this connection supplies.

Now, I'll challenge you to add more names to your list, this time using a different kind of guide. Let's see how many more points of light show up in your life with the following brain boost:

Another Look at Intimate Connection

- Daily Life Tracking Intimacy
- Family of Origin Intimacy
- Family of Choice Intimacy (i.e., surrogates)
- Shared Interests Intimacy (e.g., skiing, martial arts)
- Shared Experience (e.g., 12-step program, grew up in same city)
- Shared Values Intimacy (e.g., social causes, politics)
- Shared Association Intimacy (e.g., professional, avocational)
- Historical Experiential Intimacy (e.g., childhood friendships, traveled together, worked together on a project)
- One-time Experiential Intimacy (e.g., row companion on airplane trip)
- Ongoing Experiential Intimacy (e.g., regularly work on projects, book group, volunteer together)

If you want to go one more round of adding souls to your Intimacy Constellation (no pressure if you don't), here is one last brain boost. Using that list from the previous section on values, take a look at your top ten values and see if anyone else comes to mind. Shared Values is a very strong place to find intimate connections.

Now you are ready to personalize your Intimacy Constellation diagram. First, you need to decide what areas of connection are important to you. Go to unexpectedintimacy.com to download a free blank template or simply take a blank piece of paper and draw spokes and orbits. The diagram below has some areas identified within it that have been found to be important to many people. Use the default orbit labels or, better yet, change them so that they reflect what connections are important to you.

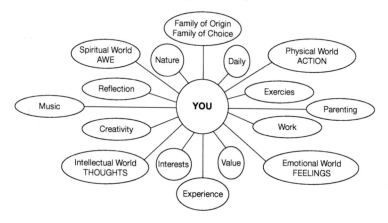

Then, one by one, place each person's name (or use their initials to save space) in and around the orbit that describes the nature of your relationship with him or her. In some orbits, experiences rather than people show up, such as the relationship between runners and the rhythm, sailors and the wind, or hikers and the forest. If you feel a deep connection and it is nourishing, put it in your constellation.

Some people may show up in more than on orbit, and that's fine. The summer conference I coordinated for twelve years is a perfect example of this (read "Belonging"). I worked with thirty-five people on the planning committee and intimate connections were found everywhere. As we worked together to create that masterpiece village experience for a large number of people, an intense shared experience ensued. I list those committee members as a group in the orbit of "Experience" Intimacy." We are connected for life.

Some of the individuals from that planning group also go in

my "Creativity" orbit (creativity is one of my strong values). That is because part of our relationship was problem-solving or program creation where we let the creative sparks fly.

Some of those same people also go in the orbit of General Emotional Intimacy. That is because either we had some immediate connection, desired to know each other more deeply, and a friendship unfolded, or we encountered some kind of conflict where we witnessed, supported, or otherwise worked through some of our own emotions with/around each other.

There are also many of these thirty-five people with whom when, during the gathering itself, our paths crossed for even a brief moment, we had a deep knowing experience of being connected to the whole. At this point in time, I no longer remember which faces I saw, but the feeling of intimate connection lingers. In the orbit of "Spiritual Intimacy," I list them, again, as a group.

It has been a few years since I worked with that planning committee, and you might question the value of listing these old connections. My rationale is that the soul part of our being doesn't keep track of time the same way as the human part of our being does. I do, on occasion, still run into someone from this group. On such occasions, I am always delighted by how good it feels for our paths to cross.

Case in point: Last month I had an email from Araya, one of the members of that planning committee. She was traveling through Asia and wondered if anyone in her circles had any Asian contacts. I emailed my beloved friend Miyuki in Japan (whom I haven't seen in more than a decade) who responded, "I'd love to have a time with person who know you! Tell her please try to call when she will arrive to Japan." Last week, I received emails from both of them. They both wrote of their own moments of unexpected intimacy. How good do I feel? Halfway around the globe my Intimacy Constellation grows brighter.

So, now it's your turn. Name your spokes and compare them with your values to make sure they are in sync. Adjust if necessary. Put your people, groups, and moments in all the orbits where you experience intimate connections with them. Watch your Intimacy Constellation unfold.

One caveat: Be careful not to start out with any judgments or expectations about how your constellation will look. There are no rules that apply to everyone. The diagram is simply a vehicle by which you can experience a fresh perspective on your own constellation of intimate connections. Balance is not the goal. The flow of nourishment and attention where it best serves your higher purpose is the goal. It is not about having an equal number of relationships in each orbit.

For example, it may be that you have five or six of points of light in "Creative Intimacy" and only two orbiting "Reflective Intimacy." But your needs for reflection are satisfied by those latter two illuminations, where it still feels like something is missing in the Creativity realm, even with five or six points of light in orbit. More dramatically, you may find a spoke that you named as important to you and find that you have *no one* in that orbit. The latter of both these cases is a signal that an opportunity for a plan of action exists.

Summary of You in the Universe

Overarching Theme
When you broaden your definition of intimacy, erring on the side of generosity, you have more points of light than you at first imagined.

Exercise for You in the Universe
1. Rank and Assess
   a. Rank the spokes in terms of what areas feel most important in your life.
   b. Look at the spoke you ranked highest and assess the quantity and quality of relationships in that orbit. Do you need more, less, or different?
   c. Are you both giving and receiving nourishment from the relationships in that orbit?
   d. Are there some connections in that orbit you want to strengthen? Do you need to adjust your expectations?

   Perform this ranking and assessment for each orbit, in the order that you ranked them. Make some notes to yourself.

2. Target Your Resources.

Identify an orbit that is important to you where you could use more/ different points of light than you currently have in your Intimacy Constellation. Go back to your list of values and activities. Take time to reflect on what you see. What needs to change? Strategize an action plan.

For example, let's say that the Spiritual Intimacy Constellation is full of experiences with nature and a few individual people. You have a sense of belonging to the Oneness of the Universe and there a few people with whom you share a sense of awe. What feels lacking, however, is a sense of belonging to something bigger than yourself. In this case, you might be a prime candidate for connecting with a group of some kind that possesses shared values.

Here's one possible strategy for achieving that aim: Either identify some individual points of light that are already in the Spiritual Intimacy orbit, or pinpoint someone in one of your other orbits whom you suspect is spiritually inclined. Be bold and ask people about the activities or groups they are involved with. Use some points-of-connection conversation (see "Social Lubrication section) but mostly engaged conversation to gain a sense of whether or not these circles would be a good fit for you.

In those conversations, you may discover groups with shared interests/values. You may also find something else: other people who are yearning for a bigger-than-self connection. After just a few of these conversations, you may even have discovered a core group that, together, can start something bigger than each of you yourselves. Be bold! Invite these people for dessert, out for coffee, or to take a walk together. Discuss ideas of what you might do together that is bigger than yourselves. Have each core person invite one or two other people.

One more example: Let's say you have defined one of your orbits with the theme of Conscious Parenting, and while a few people float around in that orbit (your partner, your parents, some friends, and a couple of books), you find your kids in a challenging new phase. That discovery makes you want to bring more light and energy to that orbit.

Here's a possible strategy: Look around you and identify some terrific kids who are the same gender but older than your own kids. The parents of those kids have already been through the phase you're going through. As such, they may have some keen insights to share. Be bold and ask for advice or at least for a few minutes of their time to reflect with you. Even humble people love to be asked for their words of wisdom. If the ages and dynamics work, you might even consider inviting the family, with their kids, for dessert or brunch, or to join you on a family adventure. Watching a family in action can prove illuminating. A side benefit of this hospitality might be the unveiling of a connection/role model for your children as they go through the next phase in their journey toward adulthood.

If that strategy feels too bold, you might consider a lower-risk one: Take a class, such as the "Love and Logic" series, instead. There, you'll meet people who share a common goal.

These two action plans are just one pair of strategies for two different orbits. Your Intimacy Constellation is unique. It is the manifestation of your own journey—what you have to offer and what your soul desires. Your commitment should be to honor that as you fill each orbit of your Intimacy Constellation with love and light.

Strategies for Choice and Change
Meeting the Challenges of the 21st Century

*The important thing is this: To be able at any moment to
sacrifice what we are for what we could become.*

~ Charles Du Bos (1882-1939), critic of French
and English literature.

WE START FORMING HABITS IN THE WOMB, and by the time we're adults, most of our habits are deeply, unconsciously ingrained in our everyday ordinary lives. While many individuals would argue that personalities don't change, we know that, hard as it is, we can change habits— especially habits we want to change.

In a comprehensive review of decades of research, we find more than a glimmer of hope. It turns out that there are only three or four significant pieces of the puzzle that, when in place, *dramatically increase the probability of successful change.* I won't keep you in suspense. Those factors are: 1) intrinsic motivation; 2) ease of access to the desired change; and 3) social support. If there is a service provider related to the new habit, then the fourth factor is having a good relationship with that provider.

Let's briefly take a look at each of these factors.

The First Rule of Success: You Gotta Wanna Do It.
If your doctor tells you that you should swim three days a week because you'll feel better if you do, but you don't enjoy swimming, then you are probably not going to do it. At the very least, you will not do it for long. Your doctor telling you to swim regularly is outside—extrinsic to—your experience. On the other hand, if you know, from your own experience, how good you feel after taking

a brisk 30-minute walk in the park down the street, you're more likely to carve out the time in your day to make that happen.

The Second Rule of Success: Use a Path That Is Already (at least partially) Cleared.

Staying with the exercise example, if the gym is on your way home from work or just around the corner from your home, then you will be more likely to go more often than you would be if it were twenty minutes out of your way. Makes sense, doesn't it? Similarly, if your Music Intimacy orbit is in need of brighter light, and you ask around at work or put up signs in the neighborhood, you'll be more likely to connect with motivated people who can find the time to join you.

Caveat for change: Try not to change too many things at once. It is best to set one goal for one change in only one area at a time.

The Third Rule of Success: Get Yourself a Buddy – Either as an Active Companion or for Regular Check-in Accountability.

In the early days of research, social support was measured as "spousal support." Thankfully, the jargon has caught up with the reality of modern Intimacy Constellations.* Now, anyone who is in your circle of support is valued. How this third rule manifests itself is that it is easier to get to the gym every Wednesday if you have made a plan to meet your friend Lorie or Henry there. Likewise, your participation in the book group is more likely to thrive if you have a buddy to drive with and everyone who attends expects (looks forward to) your presence. This social support serves as both encouragement and accountability.

---

* The findings of Liu and fellow researcher Debra Umberson of the University of Texas at Austin indicate not only a semantic change but an actual one. Their report appears in the September issue of the Journal of Health and Social Behavior. The article is called "The Times They Are a Changin': Marital Status and Health Differentials from 1972 to 2003."

The Fourth Rule of Success: Find a Provider Who Is Both Qualified and Engaged With Your Process.

Basically, this fourth rule says that when there are good connections among people, we are more motivated to make things work. If you like your personal trainer, you're more likely to "comply" with the exercise regimen. If you like the teacher of your art class, you're more likely to find a way to make it work in your schedule. If your clergyperson is an inspiring spiritual leader, you're more likely to want to get involved in activities with that community.

The Two-Pronged Challenge: Old Habits and Weak Muscles

A. Example: TV and Internet Habit

The TV/computer is in a too-convenient place and you put it on automatically.

- Cover it with an attractive tablecloth, put a piece of tape on the power button, or place the remote control out of normal reach.
- Put a piece of tape over the power button or cover it with an attractive tablecloth. That way, you have to think about it before you put it on.
- Move it into a different, off-the-beaten-path room.
- Set an alarm to limit your time.

Try this or any other strategy you can think of for one day, one week, or even one month.

B. Social Connection Muscles Weakened

Where the TV and computer are convenient and on the beaten path, our social connection skills may be a little out of practice. If that's the case for you, the research shows that you are not alone. Take one of these action steps now:

- Register
- Invite
- Volunteer
- Join
- Organize

Set Yourself Up For Success

1. Make sure whatever you choose is something you really want to do.
2. Make sure whatever you choose is not too hard or too inconvenient, and that you have access to all the information and resources you need to execute your plan.
3. Build in some form of companionship or accountability.

   Get a Buddy. Just as I found Ty, find yourself someone who shares a goal or interest. Then, keep each other going. If the issue is that you don't think you have that somebody, then use meetup.com or your local version of adult learning classes as a way to find somebody. Alternatively, ask around at work or in other circles of connection. Make it the topic you talk to everyone about. As in the case of Ty, a buddy doesn't need to be a best friend. By the way, I tried the author/book buddy once before, with someone else. It didn't take. Be bold! Don't give up if it doesn't happen on the first try. If you don't have an ongoing buddy for this, at least tell a friend or family member what you are planning to do and ask them to check in with you about it.

4. If you just can't seem to take action on your own, get a smart professional coach, one who clearly has your best interests at heart. It doesn't need to be a long-term commitment. S/he can also get you to think outside your box and help you navigate the boulders as they rise up in your path.* At least tell a friend or family member what you are planning to do and ask them to check in with you about it. A coach can provide you with some of that structure you need to get started and help you identify someone in your circles who might assume the role of buddy.

---

* I'll be happy to work with you if I have time. Contact me at author@unexpectedintimacy.com.

There now. We're done with the How To. Was it helpful? Let me know. I'd love to hear from you.

Epilogue

When the time came for me to leave the Wodaabe,
Mokao asked me to share with him the traditional
three glasses of tea: The first "strong like life," the second
"sweet like love," the third "subtle like friendship."

~ Carol Beckwith, "People of the Taboo" On the Wodaabe of Niger

THE DICTIONARY SAYS AN EPILOGUE IS A section at the end of a book that serves as a comment or conclusion to what has happened. So, what has happened in the preceding pages?

My hope is that your sense of what intimacy means has been subverted—that throughout your day, you see and feel sparks of connection and recognize them as intimate moments in a way that you never did before. My hope is that my stories will serve as a model for your own, that as you walk through your day, it is with a heightened awareness of the impact—the ripple effect— that your connections have on you and on the people around you. And better still, I hope that this awareness leads to deeper relationships where you can nourish and be nourished in everyday encounters. It might take some new skills on your part but there are many ways to learn these new skills.

One learning methodology that has been used effectively is the "See one, do one, teach one" approach. The medical community uses it to train doctors, most notably as they go through rotations and residencies. Young children, too, go through this same learning process—naturally. I remember seeing a boy who had watched his mother use a step stool to reach a high shelf, try it himself, and then show his little sister how to reach the light switch using the same approach.

Unexpected Intimacy: Everyday Connections that Nourish the Soul is the "see one"—a model for how one might experience everyday encounters as healthy, nourishing food for the soul. The "do one" is up to you. As you go through the day, think of it as a treasure hunt—bring your attention to finding the gems and jewels of personal connection. Make a list of people who are important to you. Call them or write to them and thank them for being in your life.

As a starting point to "teach one," on the next page I have included a few questions for personal reflection and discussion. I can imagine these being used as fodder for book group discussions and for parents talking with their children, and among friends—old and new—as they engage in intimate conversation. The best way to strengthen your own learning is to pass it on to someone else. With each discussion, your own ideas about intimacy and relationships will evolve. Feel free to share your insights on the website. That way, we can all keep learning.

Three Sets of Questions for Discussion and Reflection

Questions About Ideas Presented in the Book

1. After having read this book, how do you now define "intimacy"? Has your definition changed?

2. Do you feel "intimacy" is too strong, or not the right word, for some of your interpersonal connections? What term might you use instead? Why? If not, what is it that speaks to you about the term "intimacy"?

3. Did any of the stories make you laugh, cry or make you angry? Which ones resonated most strongly for you?

4. Do you believe it is possible to have an intimate connection with: Ideas? Music? Food? Land? Sacred texts? The heavens? Someone who is no longer living? Have you experienced any of these? In what way?

5. *Unexpected Intimacy* discusses various forms of spiritual, religious expression from the fixed to the creative. Do you have a sense of intimacy with a Higher Being? What brings you to that place? What do those connections add to your life? If not, do you feel it might be valuable to explore those types of intimacy? Why or Why not?

Questions To Stimulate Intimate Conversation in a Group

1. If you had the time and the support to write a book this next year, what book would you write?

2. What is one lesson you learned from your parents or from a mentor or hero (dead or alive)?

3. What is one lesson you would want to pass on to future generations?

4. If your group were to plan a full day or overnight retreat together, where would you want to go and what kinds of activities would you want do together? What role would each member play?

5. Find your own example of sharing information versus revealing feelings, similar to my example (page 210) stating that I was married to a rabbi (providing information) versus recounting the hard feelings of invisibility associated with being married to a rabbi (revealing feelings). Notice how the connections in the room change.

Questions For Personal Reflection

1. Which are the most important types of intimacy in your life? Which are the most nourishing?

2. Which types of intimacy are missing? How might you go about filling the gaps?

3. How nourishing are the encounters in your day? How often do you notice them?

4. Do you ever talk about or share your sense of intimate connections with others? If so, how does that make you and the other person feel? Is it nourishing? Uncomfortable? Why?

5. Looking beyond yourself, did reading *Unexpected Intimacy* give you any insights into needs for intimacy of your friends and members of your family that you haven't considered before?

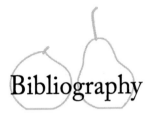

Bibliography

Beck, Martha. *The Joy Diet: 10 Daily Practices for a Happier Life.* New York: Crown Publishers, 2003.

Ben-Shahar, Tal. *Happier: Learn the Secrets to Daily Joy and Lasting Fulfillment.* New York: McGraw-Hill, 2007.

Booth, Eric. *The Everyday Work of Art: Awakening the Extraordinary in Your Daily Life.* Naperville: Sourcebooks, 1997, iUniverse, 2001.

Burt, Ronald S. *Brokerage and Closure: An Introduction to Social Capital.* New York: Oxford Press, 2005.

Covey, Stephen M. R. and Merrill, Rebecca R. *The Speed of Trust: The One Thing That Changes Everything.* New York: Free Press, 2006.

Csikszentmihalyi, Michaly. *Flow: The Psychology of Optimal Experience.* New York: Harper Collins, 1990.

Friedman, Thomas. *The World is Flat: A Brief History of the Twenty-First Century.* New York, N.Y. : Farrar, Straus and Giroux, 2007.

Gilbert, Daniel Todd. *Stumbling on Happiness.* New York: A.A. Knopf, 2006.

Gladwell, Malcom. *Blink: The Power of Thinking Without Thinking.* New York: Little, Brown and Company, 2005.

Goleman, Daniel. *Social Intelligence: The New Science of Human Relationships.* New York: Bantam Dell, Random House, 2006.

Gould, James, and Gould, Carol Grant. *Sexual Selection*. New York: Scientific American Library, 1989

Hallowell, Edward, M. *CrazyBusy - Overstretched, Overbooked and About to Snap! Strategies for Coping in a World Gone ADD*. New York: Ballantine Books, 2006.

Honoré, Carl. *In Praise of Slowness: How a Worldwide Movement is Challenging the Cult of Speed*. New York: Harper Collins San Francisco, 2004.

Jones, Shirley Ann, ed. *Simply Living: The Spirit of the Indigenous People*. Novato: New World Library, 1999.

Levine, Madeline. *The Price of Privilege: How Parental Pressure and Material Advantage Are Creating a Generation of Disconnected and Unhappy Kids*. New York: Harper Collins, 2006.

Louv, Robert. *Last Child in the Woods: Saving Our Children From Nature-Deficit Disorder*. Chapel Hill, NC: Algonquin Books of Chapel Hill, 2005.

Mashek, Debra J., and Aron, Arthur, eds. *Handbook on Closeness and Intimacy*. Mahwah: Lawrence Erlbaum associates, 2004.

Pink, Daniel, H. *A Whole New Mind: Why Right-Brainers Will Rule the Future*. New York: Riverhead Books, 2005.

Pipher, Mary. *Writing to Change the World*. New York: Riverhead, 2006.

Putnam, Robert D. *Bowling Alone : The Collapse and Revival of American Community*. New York: Simon & Schuster, 2000.

Seligman, Martin, P. *Authentic Happiness*. New York: Free Press, 2002.

Thomas, William, H. *What are Old People For?: How Elders Will Save the World*. Acton: VanderWyk & Burham, 2004.

Waters, Ethan. *Urban Tribe: A Generation Redefines Friendship, Family and Commitment*. New York: Bloomsbury, 2003

About the Author

SARAH GABRIEL IS AN EDUCATOR, COMMUNITY builder, organizational artist, and socially conscious entrepreneur. A life-long learner and world traveler, she is always observing and integrating the best life strategies from each culture and discipline she encounters.

Sarah's current interest is in the burgeoning field of Sustainable Practice which recognizes the need to integrate the knowledge and wisdom from many sources in order to keep humans happy, healthy and in balance with the rest of creation on our Planet Earth. She holds a degree in business from The Wharton School and a Master's degree from Temple University in Educational Psychology.

Sarah was born and raised in Philadelphia and has lived in Colorado since 1991. She invites readers to email her at author@unexpectedintimacy.com.